Somebody Stole the Pea Out of my Whistle

The Golden Age of Hoosier Basketball Referees

MAX KNIGHT

Guild Press of Indiana
Indianapolis

Guild Press of Indiana, Inc.
6000 Sunset Lane
Indianapolis, Indiana 46208
Tel.: 317-253-0097
FAX 317-465-1884

Library of Congress Number 95-77506

ISBN: 1-878208-62-4 (Hardcover)
ISBN: 1-878208-63-2 (Softcover)

Second Printing October, 1997.

*The inspiration for this book came
from Don McBride. The author had
planned to dedicate the book to
Don, but the Richmond referee
wished another dedication instead.
In his words . . .*

***This book is dedicated to the memory of Referee
John Hilligoss, my partner in crime for
twenty-eight years.***

— Don McBride

Contents

Acknowledgment

I am extremely grateful to Jerry Davis of Fishers, Indiana, for his time and effort in spending many hours proofreading, suggesting and generally mothering this book to its completion. His task has made my task easier.

There are others who have provided assistance. Kathleen Postle, my former creative writing teacher at Earlham College urged me to write a book for years.

Bob Showalter helped greatly in research and in proofreading the college referee chapters. Jan Clark, sports editor of *The Palladium-Item,* carefully checked the finished copy to check names and dates. Bill May made sure the right names were with the right photos. Mildred Ball, assistant commissioner of the IHSAA, has hunted names, dates and addresses for me on several occasions. Dr. Neil Thornhill of New Castle gave me the moral support needed to dig in and get the manuscript revised. Gary Fisher at Winchester went the second mile to chase down cutlines for pictures. Ron Newlin opened all doors to the Indiana Basketball Hall of Fame in our hunt for photos of referees from the Golden Age and helped tremendously in the book promotion.

Our son Eric and daughter Teresa Jackson spent hours teaching an "old dog" how to use a word processor. And a special thank you goes to my wife, Mazella, for giving me quietness in my office by answering the phone. And . . . for putting up with my mood swings.

Finally, real gratitude is double to Don McBride, not only the main character of this book, but a friend who has gone several extra miles to see this book is a success. While paying with leg pain for all those years of running backwards down a basketball floor, Don has provided the wit and good humor needed to get the Golden Age message across. He is the dean of Indiana referees.

Former IHSAA Commissioner Phil Eskew: "I saw Don McBride referee many games during his career, and I never once saw him in the wrong position to make a call. This is not a trait you learn, it is one you are born with."

Preface: Opening Tip

The idea for this book, its title and many of its stories came from retired Richmond official Don McBride. No referee in Indiana history has been more widely known in high school basketball circles around the state. Not only was he an outstanding referee, but he also put on a show as well. During a game, he talked to the coaches, he talked to the players, he talked to the fans. Many called it showboating, and it was. But the crowds loved it and very few ever took offense at his mannerisms.

It is his desire that basketball players and officials of today realize there was a time when it all was fun. It was a time when coaches and referees could lambast each other on the floor and still remain friends. An hour after a game often found coaches, referees and even sports writers, gathered around a table eating, talking and laughing together.

Former Marion Coach Woody Weir said it best. A woman fan saw Weir and McBride eating together at a restaurant after a game and said, "Coach, I am surprised you would speak to this referee." "Only away from the gymnasium, lady, only away from the gymnasium."

The Richmond official calls this era, the "Golden Age of Referees," a period from 1935 to 1980. It was in 1935 that the state tournament did away with the "Sweet Sixteen" and started using the word "Semifinals." This term lasted until 1957, when again the name was changed, this time to "Semistate." The tournament still retains this name today. In 1980 referees were instructed to tighten the game by cutting out banter with players and coaches on the floor. It totally changed the complexion of the game.

McBride knew articles and even sections of two books had been written on referees, but none had delved deeply into the subject and none had given the picture from each corner of the state. In this effort, he made sure this writer personally interviewed twenty-one former referees, as well as the winningest coach in Indiana history, Howard Sharpe at Terre Haute, and at least until now, the man most responsible for high school basketball remaining one class in our state, Milan hero Bobby Plump.

The final two chapters of the book are reserved for Indiana referees who worked college games. The remainder concerns only high schools, many long since consolidated and gone. There had to be a limit on referees interviewed, so the underlying theme of the book is this: a referee had to work with McBride to be in the flow of the story. Many other names are mentioned, but the story line follows the McBride rule. For information on these men, check the referee listing in the back of the book.

The stories are true, as each referee remembers them to be. Memory, of course, has a tendency to enhance a tale. Any discrepancies must be forgiven for, after all, fans, coaches and referees could not always agree at the moment the story happened, much less remember it the same many years later.

It is their story. They lived it . . . let them tell it.

1
The Golden Age of Referees

They came from every corner of the state of Indiana. They were bankers and farmers, teachers and laborers, insurance men and shop owners. Some were good, some only fair. None was perfect. Yet, night after night, for little pay, they gave it their all. They were the men in striped shirts who brought an added measure of enjoyment to the game of basketball. Their Golden Age now has ended. But as long as an old-timer is left to tell their stories, they will be remembered.

Don McBride was one of the best. With a whistle around his neck, tennis shoes on his feet and a love of the game in his heart, he gave an added dimension that never again will be matched. He teamed with John Hilligoss a majority of games and they made a perfect pair. McBride, outgoing, joking with the players and coaches, getting the crowd into the game, and Hilligoss, steady, quiet and the perfect ploy for many of McBride's antics.

These antics became legendary during the twenty-eight years McBride refereed, starting in 1935 and ending in 1963. The story begins during the Great Depression.

Frank Shamel, one of the state's best, knew the youthful McBride had received his license and called him to see if he could work a game with him at Centerville. The young official quickly agreed and when it was over and Shamel got his check for twenty dollars, he handed the rookie referee three dollars.

It happened again a few nights later when Shamel again asked McBride to join him, this time in a game at Lawrenceburg . . . three dollars.

A few weeks later Lawrenceburg offered McBride a game and McBride called Shamel to see if the older referee would be available to referee with him. The veteran official was open and agreed to go.

When the game was over, the principal of Lawrenceburg came to the dressing room, thanked the men for a good game and handed McBride a ten-dollar bill, a five-dollar bill and five ones. McBride turned to Shamel and said, "Thanks for a good job," and handed him three dollars. Those nearby said the air was blue for several seconds before Shamel saw the humor of the incident. The two worked several games after that, splitting the pay right down the middle.

Indiana has been fortunate in having Indiana High School Athletic Association (IHSAA) commissioners who were outstanding. None was better than L.V. Phillips. His high-pitched voice and limp handshake belied the strength of character this man possessed. When he spoke there was only one response, "Yes, sir."

In the late fifties, McBride was to officiate the final game of the Wayne County Tournament at Richmond and had gone home to get a bite to eat after the Saturday afternoon session when the phone rang. It was L.V. Phillips.

"Don," said the commissioner, "the Muncie Central at Indianapolis Tech game has been changed to tonight. The two coaches want you for that game."

"I'm sorry, Mr. Phillips," he answered, "but I have the championship game of the Wayne County Tourney tonight."

"Don," said the commissioner, "I am sure you can get another official for that game, I need you here in Indianapolis."

"But sir," the referee said, "I am obligated to fulfill my contract."

"That is not a problem," said Phillips. "I will see it is

taken care of. I will expect you over here at 7:30," and hung up.

McBride contacted Maurice (Pete) Jordan and he readily agreed to work the tourney game. Still not all was smooth sailing in spite of what the commissioner had ordered.

Charlie Dickerson, principal at Williamsburg, was tourney chairman and he was livid when he got the news. He screamed, "McBride can't do that. We've got a contract. I'll have his license for this."

Jordan did his usual outstanding job in the championship game and McBride and Marvin Todd called the Tech-Central match without a hitch. However, the commissioner either forgot or never intended to contact Dickerson to explain the change, leaving McBride out on a limb.

If this had been a situation where the principal and refreee had not been well acquainted, all contracts for the future would have been canceled. Actually, Dickerson and McBride were friends, as was Bob Warner, the Williamsburg coach. Nothing came of the incident.

But McBride could not let this one get by without pulling one on Dickerson that remains a classic.

Two weeks after the tournament, McBride and Hilligoss had the Fountain City-Williamsburg game at the Williamsburg gymnasium. Both had excellent teams and the Wayne County Conference title was at stake.

"Dickerson is still mad at me," said McBride to his partner, "so let's have some fun. I'll dress at home and stay in the car while you go to the dressing room. When you see Dickerson, tell him that since he threatened to get my license revoked, I decided to go to Cincinnati and see the Royals play. You have him call my wife to verify it and I'll get her to go along."

Hilligoss was in the dressing room, putting on his shoes, when Dickerson walked through the doorway. The conversation went like this:

"Hi John, where's McBride?"

"Oh, he said you tried to revoke his license after he went

3

to the Tech game so he isn't coming. In fact, he went to Cincinnati to see the Royals play."

"Oh come on, McBride wouldn't do that."

"All I know is, he isn't here. If you want, call his wife and check it out."

Five minutes later Dickerson came roaring back into the dressing room and he was furious.

"He's gone too far this time," he screamed. "I don't care if he's the commissioner's pet or not, I'll have his license for this. Who in the world can I get to work with you?"

"McBride said there surely would be someone in the crowd with a license. Why don't you see who you can find?"

Dickerson hurried to the gymnasium and scanned the crowd on both sides of the floor but to his dismay, he could not spot a referee. A sports writer had tipped off two who were there and they were in hiding.

Hilligoss walked onto the floor, called the captains together and when he finished with instructions, went to the scorer's bench, telling Dickerson he would have to call the game himself. The principal was jumping up and down like a kangaroo with hives, his face crimson red.

The two teams lined up for the jump and from the outside entrance doorway came McBride, bouncing the ball and blowing his whistle.

As the two teams went down the floor, Dickerson ran alongside McBride screaming, "You'll not get paid . . . you'll not get paid." But, of course, he did!

Gail (Clab) Robinson, a pioneer in refereeing, was instrumental in McBride's success, even from the early days.

"Clab taught me to think quickly, not to anticipate and always get the ball back in play as soon as possible. I picked up a lot of mannerisms from him and found out that personalities are important in officials. Also, he emphasized that appearance is vital and if you looked like an official and you appeared to know what you were doing out there on the floor, it gave you an edge. It was a lesson I never forgot."

To this good advice McBride added one element of his own, showboating. In fact, he was known around the state as the "Richmond Showboat." Calling a game was not enough; he had to be part of the game. Basketball fans loved it. So did most referees who worked with him.

The Richmond official knew many of the coaches and principals in Indiana on a first name basis and few ever marked him off their referee list. They, in turn, loved to get something back on him and often went to elaborate plans to do so.

McBride had only recently returned from service in the Marines after World War II, and had booked the Madison at Lawrenceburg game. He said it was a thrill to walk into that gymnasium and see it jammed to the rafters. The old war horse was back where he belonged, among the sweating, grunting, pounding players of basketball.

He was enjoying the moment when Lawrenceburg Principal Dwight Prather came over and said, "Hi McBride. You don't have to hurry down to dress, we have a little ceremony between games and you'll have plenty of time to get ready."

The referee told him thanks and then stood by the bleachers to watch the ceremony. It opened with the Lawrenceburg band playing, and they were good. They marched around the gym a couple times and then circled the floor as they finished their last song.

The principal walked to a microphone, which had been brought out to the center line, and asked McBride to join him.

When he got there he stopped and suddenly the band started playing, "Three Blind Mice," followed by, "When I Grow Too Old To Dream." McBride laughed along with the crowd and waved to them as they cheered. Then the referee's back stiffened and his jaw set as the band began playing the "Marine Corps March."

When the last strains of the famous march ended, the crowd roared and out of the locker room runway came a friend of McBride's, Lawrenceburg football coach Pat O'Neil. He was wearing dark glasses, carrying a white cane with a red tip and being led by a seeing eye dog.

At the microphone O'Neil said, "Don, on behalf of the basketball fans of southern Indiana, we want to present you with these trophies." With that, he handed the dark glasses and cane to the referee.

"Thank you," said McBride, "but I also want the dog." "You don't get the dog," answered O'Neil.

"But I want the dog." "Dammit, McBride, it's my dog. It's not part of the loot."

"Indian giver!" said McBride.

By this time the crowd was howling in laughter. The principal stepped back to the microphone.

"Don," he said, "we really want to present you with this plaque that says, 'To Don McBride, for outstanding officiating in basketball, from LCHS (Lawrenceburg Consolidated High School.)' Welcome back."

To this day, the Richmond official considers that evening one of the finest of his career and the plaque an honor he never expected.

Sometime later, McBride did get even with O'Neil for not giving him the dog.

Hilligoss had a microphone which when grounded, allowed a person to talk through any radio. So, McBride hooked the mike up in the shower of the Lawrenceburg dressing room and had a janitor watch for O'Neil. As the football coach came into the room, McBride "went on the air."

"Good evening ladies and gentlemen," said the voice over the radio. "This is KDKH in Pittsburgh, Pennsylvania . . . Rod O'Conner bringing you the latest off the sports wire . . . flash . . . Bear Bryant has resigned as football coach of the Kentucky Wildcats and this station has learned that Pat O'Neil, fiery coach of the Lawrenceburg, Indiana, Tigers, has been named new head coach of the Wildcats."

O'Neil stopped dead in his tracks and yelled, "Hold it, I didn't get all of that. I'd like to hear it again."

So McBride repeated it. Just then O'Neil saw Hilligoss and said, "That damn McBride is around here somewhere." He looked in the shower and there was the culprit. O'Neal reached over, flipped on the shower full force and nearly drowned the laughing referee.

Fortunately, McBride had not changed into his working outfit.

After the game, McBride and Hilligoss went to the O'Neil home for a bite to eat before heading to Richmond. They were sitting in the den eating and watching something new in most homes at that time, television, when the dog McBride had tried to con O'Neil into giving him, walked into the room.

"That sure is a fine looking bird dog," said McBride. "Is he good in the field?"

"I paid enough that he should be," answered O'Neil, "but I've had him out four times and he isn't worth the powder and lead it would take to blow him up. Birds can walk all over him and all he does is look at them."

A few minutes later the television showed hunters in an open field and suddenly a covey of quail started running across the screen. The dog leaped to its feet and made a perfect point at the television screen.

"Well I'll be damn," said O'Neil. He jumped to his feet and gave the pointer a swift kick in the rear.

McBride not only loved to pull pranks on coaches, he greatly enjoyed nailing his referee partner, Hilligoss, when he least expected it.

The two had a game at Seymour in 1957 and Hilligoss thought it odd that McBride had offered to carry both of their satchels from the car to the dressing room. He found out why when he zipped open his bag and water came pouring out. Everything was soaked, shoes, socks and athletic supporter, generally known as a jock strap.

"He squeaked up and down the floor all evening," laughed McBride.

Seymour Coach Ed Lyskowinski always had a new jock strap and socks for the referees. As he handed them to McBride, the referee said, "Oh come on Ed, you've got to do better than that if you want to win."

"Oh no, no," countered Lyskowinski, "I'm not trying to bribe you, I am simply trying to be nice." McBride said he was telling the truth, the coach was a super individual and an excellent coach.

After the game ended, Lyskowinski came into the dressing room and said, "Good game, guys. Look, you got a long drive, why don't you go down to the Elks for a sandwich before heading home and put it on my tab."

The two referees thanked him and did go to the Elks. But instead of a sandwich they both had T-Bone steaks and signed Lyskowinski's name to the bill.

The next night Seymour was at Brownstown and McBride and Hilligoss had the game. When they went to the floor, Lyskowinski came hurrying over and said, "Boy, I better win this one after seeing that dinner bill last night."

"Sure were good steaks," laughed McBride. Oh yes, Seymour lost.

With the fans on top of referees in these small gymnasiums, the officials heard all the nasty remarks tossed their way. Often McBride would joke with them and win them over. But, on occasion, there was the agitator that went too far.

The game was at Williamsburg in 1940 and a man in the front row was on the referees from the opening whistle. Nothing they called was right and "bums" was the kindest word he used. Late in the second quarter McBride had enough.

Williamsburg guard Paul (Shorty) Frazer stepped to the free throw line and as the referee handed him the ball he said, "Shorty, the next time you get the ball at the other end of the floor, throw it to me as hard as you can."

"You won't call a technical on me?" asked the player. "No," said the referee, "just toss it hard."

A few plays later, the ball ended in Shorty's hands when a foul was called. McBride stepped in front of the loud-mouth fan and Shorty heaved the ball. The referee ducked and the ball hit the fan full in the chest.

"You did that on purpose," he screamed.

With an innocent look McBride said, "I didn't throw the ball."

The fan did not say a word the rest of the way. As the two teams went down the floor McBride quietly said, "Thanks Shorty."

Referee Lowell Smith's first encounter with McBride set the tone for future games they worked together. Smith was a rookie and McBride the seasoned veteran.

The Richmond official had the Southport-Tech game at Butler Fieldhouse, now known as Hinkle Fieldhouse, but found out at the last minute the referee who was to work with him had to cancel. So the IHSAA sent Smith, a young official but one the commissioner knew was good. The year was 1954.

It was the first time Smith had worked in Indianapolis and when he walked into the dressing room there stood McBride with a scowl on his face.

"Who are you?" he asked. "Lowell Smith." "Where you from?"

"Palmyra."

"Never heard of it. Why'd they send you?"

"They couldn't get anyone else to work with you, so they called me."

"Have you worked lots of games?"

"Several, but none as big as this one."

"Now is a fine time to start. There will be seven thousand people out there tonight. Have you ever worked in front of that many?"

"Sure. As a senior I played in front of that many. You

The Whistle That Went Astray

It wasn't a pea out of a whistle that caused Don McBride a problem in the 1960 game between Muncie Central and the Anderson Indians. It was a whistle that went astray when the referee was hit in the mouth by a player's elbow. *Muncie Star* Sports Editor Bob Barnet wrote this story:

"During a tight spot in the second quarter Don detected a traveling violation and strove vainly to whistle the play dead. But he lost his whistle when hit by the player and it ended hanging down his back. Don resembled a man fighting a swarm of bees as he batted at the dangling whistle. Finally he was able to capture it, shoved it in his mouth and blew a mighty blast . . . into the wrong end.

"The referee's eyes popped, his cheeks puffed out like those of a squirrel with a double load of hickory nuts and various veins swelled dangerously in his neck.

"After several startled seconds Don finally turned the whistle around, got the right end between his teeth, and blew a somewhat weak blast that halted action.

"By this time McBride was several plays behind but he sternly marched the two teams back to the center sideline and handed the ball to a player out of bounds for the throw-in.

"Horrified denizens of the press row, seeing that McBride had lost his whistle, feared for a moment that he had swallowed it, lanyard and all." Barnet was an excellent writer. None in the state could match him for the human interest and humor he injected into coverage of a sporting event. He not only covered the Muncie Bearcats, he was a Muncie Bearcat fan.

The author remembers a statement by Barnet at the end of the Muncie-Milan game that remains a classic. Barnet had invited me, the rookie sports writer of *The Palladium-Item* to sit with him on the end of the Muncie players bench for the final game. When Bobby Plump hit his famous jumper, Barnet said, "I hate to see the Bearcats get beat, but that is the greatest thing that has ever happened to Indiana basketball." He was right!

had to total up the attendance for the entire year to make it, but there should have been seven thousand."

McBride laughed and said, "Kid, you'll do."

From that time on the two worked tourney games together and became good friends.

"I always kidded him," said Smith, "that he was the politician, the public relations man, and I did the work."

Smith used a unique method to shut up a fan, even though that fan was a friend.

"Irvin Naugle would sit at the end of the bleachers and ride me constantly, no matter what the score. He thought it was great fun, but for me, it got a little tiring. So, I decided to do something about it.

"I found an old whistle, took a pen knife and carefully whittled the wooden pea out of it. I hooked a shoestring to the whistle, stuck it in my pocket and headed for the game at Pekin Eastern.

"As I entered the gymnasium, Naugle yelled out, 'Oh, no, not you again.' I walked over to him and said, 'Irv, this is going to be a tough game, so I got this whistle for you so you can help me referee.' I handed it to him and he drew his hands back. He did not want to take it. But I insisted, reached over and draped the shoestring around his neck.

"I did not hear one word out of him the entire first half, but as I went past him to the dressing room he yelled, 'Hey Smith, somebody stole the pea out of my whistle.' I looked back at him and yelled, 'Blow harder!'

"It sure did shut him up," said the referee.

Until consolidation of schools in the sixties, the small gymnasiums often presented a physical hazard as well as the closeness of the crowd. Sometimes the hazard appeared totally unexpected.

Referee Karl Bly, who tipped the scales at two hundred twenty pounds, was working with McBride at Brownsville in Union County. Heat for the gymnasium came through a grate between the wall and the out-of-bounds line, right at the center circle. Each time Bly crossed the grate it would bounce and the noise could be heard throughout the gym.

In the third quarter, just as he reached the floor grate, play shifted and Bly made a fast stop but the floor grate did not. It went flying off the hole and the referee caught himself as he started to fall through. Bly received a skinned leg from the accident, but had he fallen into the shaft, he could have been seriously injured.

There were occasions in years long gone by when refinished gymnasium-floors became skating rinks due to the wrong material being used to clean them. But only once has it been reported that a janitor, innocently running his wide dust collector mop during halftime, caused a major problem.

The game was at Sand Creek in Decatur county and Fred Marlow had the contest with John Thomas. Because of consolidation the game was being played in a new gym and the first half went off without a hitch.

Everything looked normal as the janitor finished his halftime chore of dusting off the floor, a maneuver used by all schools during the mid-game break.

"We headed back to the floor for the second half," said Thomas, "just as the Sand Creek team came running in from the corner entranceway. The first player's feet went straight into the air and he fell on his back. Before they could get stopped, half the team was piled around him and the others were skidding across the floor like ice skaters.

"The Sand Creek coach, Dave Porter, who later had some fine teams as coach of Jac-Cen-Del, was dumbfounded until a red-faced janitor came hurrying over and said he had accidentally picked up the mop they used to oil the school floors each evening. There was only one thing to do. Janitor, coaches, players, student managers, yell leaders and referees got down on their hands and knees with rags and wiped the oil off the floor. The game was delayed almost twenty minutes and there still were some slick spots. If a player skidded, we simply ignored it."

Karl Bly's first game with McBride in 1948 contained the funniest moment of his career, and the referee still wipes tears each time he tells the story.

"The game was at Brownsville and McBride had only recently returned from the Marines. Later, very few things got to him, but that night it happened.

"It was late in the third quarter and the game had been rough from the word go. But the worst thing was, some guy in the Brownsville section was giving us fits. You could hear his voice above everyone else and he got rough in his language. We had talked about it at halftime and decided the best thing to do was get the game over and get out of there.

"Then this guy really got on McBride, challenging his ancestry and a few other things. Don had all he could take. He blew his whistle to stop action and went bounding into the bleachers. People got out of the way as McBride yelled, 'Who is it up here that doesn't like the way we are calling them. Stand up you coward.'

"So help me," said Bly, "when this guy stood up he was the Philistine giant all over again. He must have been 6'--7" and three hundred pounds, all muscle. McBride looked at him, and you could hear a pin drop as he yelled, 'All right. I want all the rest of you people up here to shut your mouths but,' he said, pointing at the huge fan, 'mister, you holler all you want to.' "

Winfield (Dick) Jacobs learned early the respect the IHSAA office had for McBride as a referee.

The game had College Corner at Liberty in Union County in the early fifties, and Bill Curry was coach of the home team. It had been an excellent ball game for three quarters, but early in the fourth, there was a huge pile-up of players near the Liberty bench.

"Both McBride and I blew our whistles to stop action and began to unpile the players," said Dick. "As we did, Don said, 'There has to be a foul in here someplace and we are going to put it on you.' He pointed at the Liberty center, their star player, who was on the bottom of the pile.

"Since that fouled his center out of the game, Curry was furious. The next morning Curry called L.V. Phillips at the IHSAA office in Indianapolis and reported what had happened, including McBride's remark.

"The line was dead for a moment," said Jacobs, "and then the commissioner said, 'Coach, that is just one of the breaks of the game when you hire McBride.'"

Many referees, as well as players, often smacked into the double firedoors most small gyms were required to have under one basket, causing them to pop open. Hoping it would happen and then seeing that it did, gave Lawrenceburg Coach Bud Bateman a chance to get one on McBride.

The referee was going backwards at full speed when he hit the crash bar on the double doors and out into a bank of snow he went. Bateman had two men standing in waiting. Before McBride could right himself the men slammed both doors shut. McBride pounded on the door but no one would open it. So he hurried around the building to the gymnasium entrance and as he entered the woman at the counter asked, "Do you have a ticket, Mr. McBride?"

"No, of course not. I'm one of the referees."

"Mr. Bateman said no one gets in without a ticket."

"But I'm the referee."

"Can't help it. You got to have a ticket. Mr. Bateman's orders."

Just then, McBride saw Bateman peeking around a corner at him and he realized his conversation with the woman had gone out over a loudspeaker. He re-entered the gymnasium to the laughing roar of the crowd.

Fred Marlow also got in trouble while going backward at full speed to cover a play in a 1960 game.

"The game was at Logansport," said Marlow, "and I was at the edge of the out-of-bounds line, near the center of the floor. As the out official it was my job to get under the basket on a fast break and that is what I was doing.

"Suddenly I rammed full tilt into a young woman and an entire tray of Cokes went flying into the air, over me, over the girl, over the floor and a couple of front row fans. It was a junior selling Cokes and she had just stepped onto the floor from the bleachers and did not see me coming.

"It took us a good five minutes to clean up the mess and I had to contend with sticky Coke on my shirt the rest of the game."

The Milton gym in Wayne County actually was a stage sitting four feet above the level of the seats. It was open to the seats but closed by walls on three sides. The distance from the out-of-bound's line to these walls was two feet.

Referee Jim Ridge was working with McBride, and on a fast break a Milton player threw a pass directly at the Richmond official. He ducked and the ball bounced off the wall and into the hands of a player who laid it up for two points. No call.

At the next time-out, Ridge came over and said, "Hey dummy, didn't you see that ball hit the wall."

"Sure," replied McBride, "I ducked, didn't I."

"Yeh, but it still was out of bounds."

"I thought it was a beautiful pass," laughed McBride, walking away.

The Economy gym, also in Wayne County, was as small as the one at Milton, but it was in a separate building from the school and had a roof that leaked every time it rained. Ridge called a foul on a Webster player, and as the Economy boy stepped to the line, Ridge felt a drop of water hit his head. As a natural reaction he looked up and the next drop hit him square in the eye. He said he refereed the next five minutes with blurred vision.

Jim Howell was in his last game as a coach at Centerville in Wayne County and the game was at Boston. He planned to enter administrative work and Ridge knew about it. In all of his years of coaching, Howell, who was an excellent small-school coach, had not personally received one technical foul. Ridge told the players on the floor what he was going to do since Centerville had a big lead and there was only a minute to play.

The ball went out of bounds near the Centerville bench and Ridge blew it dead. He then walked over to Howell and said, "I understand you have never had a technical. Well, you have now." Pointing at Jim and then crossing his flat hand over his extended fingers he shouted, "That's a T!"

Howell looked at him in dismay and asked, "What in the world is that for?"

"It's for doing nothing," answered Ridge, and Boston shot the free one and took the ball out of bounds.

There were times when the small gymnasium proved a help to coaches, although in this case the coach could not believe it was happening to him. McKinley was playing at Spartanburg in Randolph County and the host team was well known for its fiery coach Tracy Turner. Turner and McBride had known each other since childhood in Richmond, but that made no difference during a game.

Late in the third quarter McBride called a foul on a Spartanburg player at the McKinley free throw line. The referee signaled the call and turned toward the basket. Suddenly he realized that Turner was right behind him, screaming and windmilling his arms.

"Trace," asked the referee, "what are you doing out here?" The Spartanburg coach kept right on raving.

"Trace, you know you are not allowed on the floor to protest a call. It's going to cost you a T for every step from here to the bench and don't try and get your players to carry you."

Turner stopped shouting, looked at McBride and said, "You can't do that."

"The hell I can't," McBride answered.

Turner made it from the foul line to the bench in three giant steps with McBride motioning a technical for each step. The McKinley player shot four free throws and got the ball out of bounds.

In another game at Spartanburg, McBride called a last-second foul and Turner's team lost by one point. The coach came roaring into the dressing room after the game and jumped all over the second referee, Bill Berry.

"Hey Trace," said McBride, "I made the call, not Bill. Why are you jumping all over him?"

Turner looked at McBride, grinned and said, "It wouldn't do any good to jump on you, you would just ignore it."

New referees worked the small schools in order to get known and to have a chance to move up to the bigger games. But the veterans also liked to work the small school games, for it was there they could have the closeness with fans and coaches that simply did not happen at the big schools.

Because he was part of the crowd in those small gymnasiums, a referee had to have a sense of humor and a long fuse or he did not last. He also had to be quick on the uptake, and most referees agreed, it was as hard to work at the small gyms as it was the big fieldhouses. But it was more fun.

Coaches also had to coach differently on the small floors. When they hit the bigger floors, shooting percentages took a drastic drop. Many never figured out why.

The Randolph County Tournament was being held at the big Ball State college gymnasium. Spartanburg was a strong favorite, but its shots over the opposing team's zone defense were falling short. At halftime, Turner walked over to McBride and asked, "What are we doing wrong? We hit .500 at home and .200 here."

"Your players are used to a small floor. They are shooting from farther out without realizing it. Have them move one step closer."

Turner got his chalkboard out and showed them what McBride was talking about. It worked beautifully and the Tomcats won the tournament over McKinley, 34-28.

As the game ended, McBride and Turner were walking off the floor side by side when the referee said, "Trace, send me half your paycheck for coaching."

"You send me half of yours," the coach replied. "When you're calling a game, I always do a lot more refereeing than you do."

In another confrontation between McBride and Turner, the coach came out the winner, although he never got the Richmond referee to admit it.

Just as a Spartanburg player was tossing the ball in bounds, the other team called time out and McBride whistled the ball dead. Turner leaped off the bench and yelled, "McBride, you can't do that. The ball was in play."

McBride walked over to Turner and said, "Why not? Turn to page 36, rule 17, the fourth line, and you will see I am right."

Turner, who could quote the rule book line for line, said, "McBride, what are you trying to pull? There is no rule on page 36 that has anything to do with your call."

McBride grinned and said, "Maybe it is page 37." He never admitted to Turner he had made it up.

Turner's team was playing at Ridgeville and the game ball seemed dead. The coach called Referee Jim Ridge over and said, "Blow up that game ball. It isn't bouncing right." Ridge explained there were dead spots on the floor and bounced the ball on one to demonstrate. Turner, always quick on the comeback said, "We'll be playing most of our game on the dead spots, so blow up the ball."

The most famous small-school team in Indiana will always remain the Milan Indians. Milan's Bobby Plump says the Indians overcame the small-floor syndrome to win the state title by having to lose on the big floor at Butler. It took that for them to get over the overwhelming feeling of the place.

"We were fortunate enough to have a team in the state finals two years in a row," said the Milan star. "This had not happened before, nor since, to a small school like ours. When we walked into Butler Fieldhouse in 1953, no one on the team had seen, much less played, on a floor of that magnitude. But when we were fortunate enough to get back there one year later we knew what to expect."

It is interesting to note, Plump, Ray Craft, Gene White and the rest of the Milan state champions agree that their game against Muncie Central for the state title was the poorest game they played in the entire tournament. Not until halftime was there any intent on holding the ball, as Plump did. Poor shooting by the Indians brought on the cat-and-mouse game.

"But," said Plump, "we won, and that is what counts."

As *Indianapolis Star* sports writer Bob Collins often said, "Had Bobby Plump missed that last shot, today he would be pumping gas in Pierceville." Somehow that is doubtful, but there is no doubt his "shot heard round the world" for a 32-30 win over the mighty Bearcats will never be forgotten by Hoosier fans.

Relationship Rule

Don McBride, Charlie Fouty, Cy Birge and many other referees agree that the relationship rule that came into effect in 1980 took a tremendous part of basketball camaraderie out of the game. Here is that rule.

Relationships With Players and Coaches: "The official's relationship with coaches and players should be dignified, courteous and, to a large degree, quite impersonal. His or her attitude should be such as to command respect. The official should generate a feeling among coaches and players that he or she knows what to do and is interested in providing the best possible atmosphere for a well-played game. Toward the players, the official will be neither arrogant nor patronizing. 'Kidding' a player has no place in the game; neither does a belligerent attitude. After a game, the official will neither seek out nor deliberately avoid the coach. If necessary, the official will answer questions in a courteous manner but will always avoid any arguments or confrontations with either players or coaches."

Chiding a coach, chatting with the fans and encouraging a player on the floor were a vital part of the Golden Age, now gone. No longer can a referee pull off a "McBride speciality." Union City was at Lynn and McBride had the game. With the score tied and two seconds to go in overtime, a Union City player was fouled. When he stepped to the line to shoot a free throw, McBride handed him the ball and said, "Son, relax and hit it. It's time to go home." The kid canned it dead center.

Referee Charlie Northam had battled Williamsburg Coach Bob Warner throughout the entire evening. Late in the game Northam called a foul on Williamsburg's star center that sent him to the bench. When the referee approached Warner the coach said, "Charlie, you have to be the worst referee in the state."

After the game, referees, coaches, sports writers and friends gathered at Warner's for snacks and basketball talk. Warner said for all to hear, "Charlie, you do a damn good job."

"Hey, Bob," said the referee, "an hour ago I was the poorest referee in the state." "Yeh," answered Warner, "but that was before we won!"

Don McBride nails a player for an illegal pick in a 1960 game at Indianapolis. When McBride made a call, he left no doubt as to the type of infraction committed.

-**Star** *photo by Frank H. Fisse*

Referee George Bender watches a shot taken by Terre Haute Garfield great Clyde Lovellette at Butler University during the 1947 championship game. Garfield lost to Shelbyville, 68-58.
 -Photo courtesy Indiana Basketball Hall of Fame

Liberty Coach Harry Brandley, second from left, had two working officials and two visiting officials searching the rules book for an answer prior to the start of a game. The referees are, (l-r) Burl Shook, Ross Dorsett, John Hilligoss and Tom Baker.
 -Photo courtesy Indiana Basketball Hall of Fame

Referee Wilbur May readies to point at Richmond center Milo Beam(45), as he calls a personal foul in this fifties action. The hands on his hips indicate Beam did not agree. The second referee, with the ball, is Charlie Northam.

    -Richmond Palladium-Item *photo*

Dark uniforms were common for referees to wear in the early nineteen forties. The shirts were broadcloth and both referees working a game had to wear the same color shirt. However, the men did not have to wear matching trousers as these three show, waiting for the start of the 1946 state tournament at Butler Fieldhouse. The referees are, (l-r) C. N. Phillips, Walter Thurston and George Bender.
-Photo courtesy Nancy Phillips Bassett

Referees Nate Kaufman and Carl Burt work the afternoon game of the 1937 state finals in packed Butler Fieldhouse. Huntingburg defeated Fort Wayne Central, 30-28, but lost to Anderson in the championship game.
-Photo courtesy Indiana Basketball Hall of Fame

Richmond Athletic Director Lyman Lyboult talks with referees
Charlie Northam, seated on the table, and Wilbur May prior to a
1953 game at Civic Hall in Richmond.
        -Richmond Palladium-Item *photo*

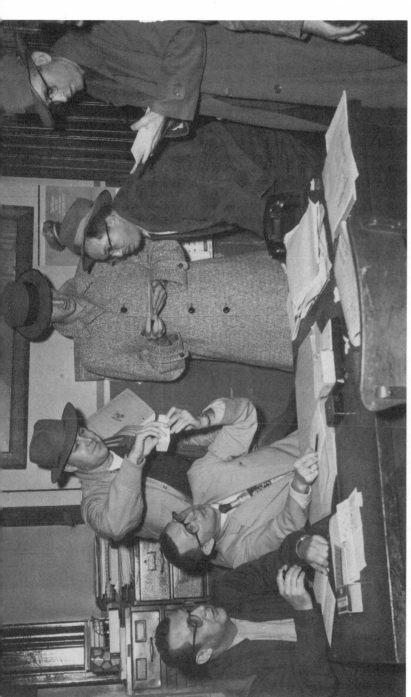

Coaches and principals met with Randolph County Superintendent Paul Beck, seated second from left, to draw for the 1956 county tournament. Seated far left is Bob Jones while standing, (l-r) are Keith Helms, Fred Powell, Robert Egly and Willie Satkamp.

-Richmond Palladium-Item photo

In this early sixties photo, Referee Glen Wisler attempts to explain a call to a player. The young man tries to tell the official why he feels it should have gone the other way. Guess who won the debate?
-*Photo courtesy Glen Wisler*

27

Officials row at the 1953 Winchester Sectional. Front row, (l-r) Dwight Dickey, sports writer; George Frazier, tourney official; Gary Fisher, timekeeper; Joe Scher, timekeeper; Kenny Poucher, scorekeeper and Walter Brumbaugh, tourney official. Second row (l-r), the author and his wife, Mazella and Max Knight, then a reporter; Phil Smith, reporter; Don Busick, tourney official; Jim Wall, announcer, and Don McHolland, assisting the announcer.
-Richmond Palladium-Item photo

In a 1955 tournament at Farmland, Randolph County, the three referees, Karl Bly and Jim Ridge, left, and Oscar Samuels, right, presented the two coaches for the final game, Keith Helms, center left, and Lloyd Mitchell, center right, with crying towels. It was all in good fun and could not be done under today's rules.

-Richmond Palladium-Item photo

Referee Ed Strathmiller keeps a close eye on a Jefferson of Randolph County defender as Jerry Ellis of New Castle goes up for two points, New Castle won the 1949 state semifinal game, 49-43.

-Photo courtesy Indiana Basketball Hall of Fame

2

Referee View of Milan Victory

Reams of paper have been used to describe the Muncie Central-Milan game of 1954. Ask any basketball fan in Indiana who hit the shot heard round the world and the answer is immediately, "Bobby Plump." Fans still refer to that year's state champions as, "The Mighty Mites of Milan," or "The Mighty Men of Milan," or even "The Giant Killers."

There were two referees working that historic game. These men have never been asked their feelings, nor their thoughts, as the game ran down and the shot was taken. One, Marvin Todd, passed away in 1992. The other, Cyril (Cy) Birge, still remembers. Here is his story:

"I had officiated for twenty-five years when I got the 1954 final game assignment. In 1951, I had worked the afternoon game of the finals between Muncie Central and Lafayette Jeff, along with Robert Hoffman. I was back in 1952, again an afternoon game between Indianapolis Tech and Lafayette Jeff, and John Hilligoss was assigned as the second official. Under IHSAA rules at that time, two final assignments were all a referee was allowed.

"Todd had worked two games in the finals, the second game of the afternoon between Jasper and Auburn in 1949, [Roland Baker was the second official], and the championship game in 1950 with Jack O'Neal when Madison defeated Lafayette Jeff for the title.

"But in 1954, the IHSAA changed the rules, allowing a referee to work three state finals and I was assigned the final game with Todd.

"Sure, I had read about Milan in the newspaper. Marvin Wood had done a good job down there, and since his team was from a school of only 161 students, all the papers carried the story.

"While we were getting dressed for that final game, neither Todd nor I said a word about either team. I do not know why, but in my mind I was expecting a slow-moving game. Neither Milan nor Muncie were known to run slow offenses, but the feeling was there. I also knew sometimes that type offense is harder to referee than a fast paced game. After a player holds a ball for two or three minutes, you have a tendency to ask yourself, has he already dribbled? Will he automatically move his feet before placing the ball on the floor, due to standing in one spot so long? Which foot was his pivot foot when he stopped? Many thoughts went through my mind.

"The game started and no one showed signs of a slow game, but neither team was tearing up the nets. This lasted the entire first half and it was a low-scoring contest.

"In the dressing room we talked about the poor shooting and I became fully convinced the cat-and-mouse game was coming. Sure enough, as soon as the ball was tipped, the slowdown started.

"But, even with the slow pace, a referee cannot let up one moment. Players on both teams were moving in and out from the basket, even as the ball was being held at center court. And you must watch for an air double-dribble, a rule few fans realize even exists.

"An air dribble occurs when the player holding the ball switches the ball from one hand to the other in the air.

"If he has his hand on the ball when he moves it, it is not a dribble. But if he tosses the ball from one hand to the other, it is the same as putting it on the floor. He can do it once, the same as a dribble, but if he does it a second time,

Few Knew Air Dribble Rule

In the 1954 Milan-Muncie Central state finals, one of the biggest worries of the two referees was whether Bob Plump, holding the ball at center court for over four minutes, would air dribble. If he had done so, the ball would have gone out to Muncie and who knows what might have happened.

Plump did not air dribble, but it was not because he was making sure he did not. It was pure luck. He never heard of the rule until it was called to his attention during the writing of this book.

The air dribble was put into the rule book in 1935 when the revised dribble definition regarding control of the ball went into effect. If a player tossed the ball in the air from one hand to the other while the player was standing motionless it was considered the same as putting the ball on the floor, a dribble. If he tossed it back to his other hand it was a violation or double dribbling. Also, after tossing the ball from one hand to the other the player then puts the ball on the floor to dribble, it is a violation for he technically has dribbled the ball twice, double dribbling.

This rule lasted until 1969 when the new rule simply said, "air dribble eliminated." Oddly enough, the first rule change made by Dr. James Naismith one year after he invented the game in 1892, was the legalization of an air dribble. A player could not move either foot as the ball was passed from one player to another or a shot taken, but the new rule allowed the ball to be moved from hand to hand to try and confuse the defender. The rule lasted forty-three years.

it is double dribbling. I was quite happy neither Marvin nor I had to make such a call for the fans would have gone berserk. And I later found out from Plump that he had never heard of the rule and considered it plain luck he did not air dribble by mistake.

"I remember looking at the scoreboard soon after the fourth quarter started and seeing the game was tied. There had been very few fouls that far [ten on Muncie and four on Milan], and not many held-ball situations. Muncie scored and Milan brought the ball to center court where Plump took a pass and stopped.

"I must admit you could feel the tension in the air as Plump stood at the center circle for over four minutes, holding the ball, first in front of him, then under his arm and finally with both hands extended. But he did not air dribble. The score then was 28-26 in favor of Muncie.

"Out of the corner of my eye, I saw Muncie Coach Jay McCreary sitting with both feet on top of a basketball, seemingly very calm. At that moment, Milan Coach Marvin Wood motioned to his players for a time-out and one of them [Ray Craft] signaled me. Todd and I blew our whistles in unison and called the break.

"When play resumed, Milan worked the ball to the corner and Plump got a good shot . . . but missed. Muncie pulled in a clean rebound and started a fast break, but a Milan player blocked off the Muncie guard and he threw the ball away.

"Todd handed the ball to Milan in front of the Milan bench and down the floor they came. This time a Milan player [Craft] drove for the basket, laid up a shot and it went in. A Muncie boy tried to block the attempt and came within a hair's breath of fouling the shooter. But he did not. The score was tied again.

"Muncie took its time getting down the floor, but again a bad pass cost them and Milan had the ball. This time Plump headed up a fast break and, although he missed the shot, was fouled. As the down official I tossed the ball to Todd and he handed it to Plump. Marvin said something to the shooter, I never knew what. Plump grinned and hit both free tosses.

"Again Muncie lost the ball and a Milan player [Craft] missed a wide-open lay-up, although he did have a Muncie player bearing down on him. No foul, however. This time down the floor Muncie scored [Gene Flowers] and the score was tied again.

"I do not know who brought the ball down court as I went under the basket to cover my position. But after crossing the ten-second line I saw Milan [Craft] signal time-out to Todd and when I glanced at the clock, it showed eighteen seconds to play and the score, 30-30. Marvin and I did not talk during that time-out.

"Plump passed the ball to a Milan player [Craft] and got it right back. I was watching the players move and realized that all but Plump were on my right side. The Muncie defense went with them, leaving one Milan player [Plump] and one Muncie player [Barnes] to my left.

"I had no idea how many seconds were left [five], when Plump faked to my right, his left, and drove toward the basket. I saw the shot go up from the corner of my eye and glanced up to see it hit dead center. Both my arms immediately went into the air.

"A Muncie player grabbed the ball, jumped out of bounds, threw it in, and before anyone could catch it, the horn sounded. I did not touch the ball after Plump scored.

"No, I did not know the significance of the game at that moment. Sure, the crowd was going wild, but Todd and I quickly headed for the dressing room. Our job was finished.

"We congratulated each other on a good game and sat down to relax before taking a shower. It was then we talked about the game, but again, from our standpoint as referees. After a few minutes we showered and were about dressed when the first visitor entered the officials room. It was Muncie Coach Jay McCreary. He shook our hands and told us we had done an excellent job of officiating.

"On our way out of the fieldhouse, Marvin Wood came running over and he was so sky high he said, 'Thanks fellows, you did a fine job,' and off he ran.

"But for both Todd and myself, the letter we received from the IHSAA office a few days later is a valued keepsake.

On behalf of the board of controls, assistant commissioner Robert S. Hinshaw and myself, I wish to express our sincere thanks for the very fine job you performed in officiating the final game of the tourney last Saturday. We are inclined to agree with what appears to be the unanimous opinion of the public that our 1954 final basketball tourney was the greatest ever. Several records were broken, not the least of which is the fact that to date, we have not heard or read a single complaint about the officiating in any of the three games. Congratulations are in order for every one of you six officials who contributed so much to our very successful tournament. Sincerely, L.V. Phillips, commissioner.

"Neither Marvin nor I had any idea the impact this game would have on Indiana basketball. To us it was simply another game, although pressure-packed due to its being the final game of the state tourney. A good official learns not to get worked up over any winner, even Milan."

Birge did not see Bobby Plump again until a year later. "I went to Butler to work an early-season college game with DePauw. Both teams were in the dressing room for last-minute instructions when I came onto the floor. There was a young man sweeping the floor before the start of the game, and I thought he looked familiar. When he reached the other end and turned around, it was Plump. He saw me, as he came back up the floor, and waved. I learned Plump had been ill and forced to miss the first few games of the season.

"During his four years of varsity at Butler, I refereed several games in which he played. We became very good friends, and remain so today."

One last note on the Muncie-Milan game.

Jay McCreary was sitting in an Indianapolis restaurant after the upset, and a stranger walked up to his table.

"Did you see the Muncie-Milan game?" he asked, not recognizing the coach.

"Yes I did," McCreary answered.

"Well I'll tell you one thing," the man said. "If I was Jay McCreary of those powerful Muncie Bearcats, and I let a little school like that beat me, I would go out and cut my throat."

McCreary leaned back in his chair, threw his head back and showed the man his throat.

A look of recognition came over the stranger's face. He said, "Oh, my God," and hurried away.

There is an unwritten code that says referees are not supposed to root for any team, but there are times when this rule is overlooked. This was a case of one coach trying to get one referee and the referee won out. It happened in 1953.

Lafayette was at Shelbyville and McBride and Hilligoss had the game. Coach Frank Barnes had his Shelbyville team three points ahead with fifty-five seconds to play and the ball was theirs under the Lafayette basket.

But, as they came up the floor, the Shelbyville guard was dribbling the ball high when Lafayette guard Denny Blind, now principal at Jeff, flipped the ball away, got control, drove for the basket, hit the lay-up and Hilligoss called a foul on Shelbyville.

When McBride turned to the bench to signal the foul, Coach Barnes came running onto the floor.

"Hey, Frank," yelled McBride, "where are you going?" "I'm going to get Hilligoss." "But you're on the floor." "Yeh, and its my floor."

"No, Frank," said the referee, "for thirty-two minutes it is mine and you are on my floor."

With that, Barnes shoved McBride, and started to pass. "Frank," said McBride, "I hate to tell you this, but you just committed a criminal offense. That is going to cost you one," and he whistled a technical.

Blind stepped to the line, hit the free throw to tie it and then the second one to put them ahead by one. The ball went to Jeff out of bounds and they ran out the clock for the one-point win.

McBride and Hilligoss got a police escort out of town and never refereed for Barnes again.

McBride knew his call was right, although Barnes became a sworn enemy. At the semifinals that year the Richmond referee was assigned to Indianapolis and Shelbyville won its regional. Barnes called the IHSAA office and asked which game McBride was on. Phillips told him he would find out when he got to Butler Fieldhouse the same as everyone else.

Shelbyville faced Milan and McBride was not assigned to that game. So, wearing his white jacket over his striped shirt, the Richmond referee decided to watch the game and sat directly in front of the Milan fans. Since the Indian colors were black and gold, the white jacket stood out like a sore thumb.

In the first half Milan only allowed Shelbyville two field goals. On the way to the dressing room, McBride made sure he got directly behind Coach Barnes when he shouted, "That is the first time I ever saw a team not only eat the ball but get it crammed back in when it tried to come out."

The Shelbyville coach saw Commissioner Phillips between games and told him of McBride's remark. He demanded that McBride be disciplined for making it.

Phillips said, "Coach Barnes, how can I discipline someone for telling the truth?"

The next day, McBride's telephone rang at Richmond and it was the commissioner's office.

"If you are over this way in the next couple days," said Phillips, "stop in."

"Yes, sir," answered the referee.

Realizing all the state tournament games were filmed,

McBride did not know what to expect. After all, he did root for Milan.

When he walked into the office he saw a projector set up and the commissioner said, "I have something to show you."

Sure enough, it was the Milan-Shelbyville game and the first shot of the crowd showed some silly-looking character, in a white jacket, leading the yells for Milan.

"I also wanted Milan to win," said the commissioner, "but I wasn't out there leading yells. In the future, restrain yourself." Enough said.

Do referees ever favor one team over another? Not often, but it does happen.

The Indiana School for the Deaf at Indianapolis had never won a sectional game. Its chance came in 1952.

McBride refereed the game with Burl Shook from Richmond. As it progressed, McBride later said it was impossible not to get caught up in it and to root for the Deaf School. Did this cause the referees to lean calls toward the school without actually meaning to do so?

"Yes," the referees admitted. "In fact, the opposing coach came up to us after the Deaf School won and said, 'thanks for nothing.' "

The next night the Deaf School played Attucks and got clobbered.

Several high school referees also worked college games for extra income. One who had great success was Cy Birge, starting in state conferences and ending with eleven years as a Big Ten official.

But his love remained with high school basketball, despite all the success he had working college games. He loved the association with the coaches and players, something he could not have in the Big Ten.

"I cultivated friends like Odon's Joe Todrank," said Birge, "but during a game, friendships were forgotten and we both did our jobs as we best saw fit. In fact, Joe learned the hard way that this was true.

"The game was at Monroe City, a small gymnasium, and each time I came past the Odon bench, Todrank was standing up, causing me to duck around him. After the second time I said to him as I went past, Joe, get in your seat or there will be problems.

"A few minutes later, down came Odon on a fast break and there was Joe directly in my path. So, I whistled the ball dead and put a technical on him.

"After the game Joe came into the dressing room. I said, I kept telling you to sit down or there would be trouble. He laughed and said, 'Yeh, but I didn't think you had guts enough to call it.' "

"Joe," said Birge, "you all look alike when you are out there on the floor."

A mid-fifties game at the Purdue Fieldhouse between Lafayette Jeff and Gary Roosevelt must have ended the right way. Birge was darn glad it did. "Those two teams went at it tooth and toenail," said the referee, "and the fans were hostile to say the least. We were glad when it was over and even more glad when a Jeff official told us that a loaded pistol had been found lying on the floor in the cheering section."

The next year, Birge did run into a buzzsaw with another Gary team, Froebel. The game was the semifinals at Lafayette and Gary was leading, 43-38, in the third quarter when Birge ejected two Froebel players during a time span of two minutes.

"Both players committed flagrant fouls, far beyond reason, and I ousted them. A few minutes later a third player for Froebel also committed a flagrant foul. I did not toss him out, but I did give him a technical.

"As you can imagine, the Froebel crowd wanted my head.

"I never have heard such booing nor name calling as I heard during that game. Jeff won, 71-58, and went on to the final game of the state, losing to Attucks.

"Froebel protested my calls to the commissioner and Phillips informed the school the next week, prior to the finals, 'The decision by Birge was correct.' The Gary school officials sent a letter to the IHSAA office saying it might join a conference in Michigan and get out of the Indiana tournament. After reading the letter, Phillips remarked, 'That might not be a bad idea.' "

There were coaches throughout the state who were well known for their fiery tempers and intimidating antics. None could hold a candle to Johnnie Baratto at East Chicago. He often fired up his team by getting a referee to call a technical. Yet, if there was a problem that should not have been, Baratto could show a different side. Referee Bob Spay tells this story:

"Baratto's team was playing Michigan City in the regional and in the third quarter an East Chicago player fouled a Michigan City boy as he went in for a lay-up. The kid hit the basket and I whistled a foul, but it didn't end there. The East Chicago guard shoved the shooter well into the end bleachers and I immediately hit him with a technical.

"Baratto came hurrying onto the floor," Spay continued, "and I said, John, I know you couldn't see this, but your boy shoved the shooter five rows into the bleachers."

"What was that kid's number?" asked the East Chicago coach. "I want him out of there right now."

"You will have plenty of time," Spay answered, "for I am going over and tell the bench what happened and get me a shooter."

Suddenly, both Baratto and Spay could hear the East Chicago radio announcer yelling into his microphone, "Coach Baratto is all over the referee for that last call. He really is letting the official have it."

Baratto looked at Spay and said with a grin, "You go straighten out that dumb announcer and I'll go get my kid and set him on the bench."

"Baratto wanted everything he could get in a ballgame," said the Kokomo official, "but he knew the rules, was an excellent coach and a likeable guy."

A conversation between Baratto and McBride sets the pattern for officiating, no matter where it is in the state of Indiana. Baratto told the official he liked to bring his team to the center of the state to play during the season so the players could get use to the different type refereeing from up north.

"Why?" asked McBride. "Do they call them different up north?"

"Yes, they let us play. There are not as many fouls called." "Do you think we make up the fouls?" "No, I am not saying that."

"If you go by the rule book, John, there should not be a difference. And that is all any official should follow."

"But different officials have different interpretations," said Baratto.

"That may be true," answered the referee, "but if you go strictly by the book, you do not need an edge. John, a charge is a charge, a block is a block, a travel is a travel and a hack is a hack. The only difference is why a charge is a charge, why a block is a block, why a travel is a travel and why a hack is a hack. Officials must be sure and interpret correctly, according to the rules, and not make it up as they go."

"Would you agree with me that blocking and charging are the two most controversial calls?" asked Baratto.

"Most certainly," answered McBride, "along with the failure to call an intentional foul at the end of a game.

"Also," McBride added, "the rule book says that a player must not put his hand inside the goal on a shot or the shot is not counted. Is it ever called? No. But you tell me how you are going to dunk the ball without getting your hand inside the cylinder?"

Barrato shrugged and said with a grin, "Mac, it boils down to this. I'll play them the best I know how and you call them the best you know how. Between us we'll give the fans a show." There is no doubt. Of all the coaches and referees in the business, none gave a better show than McBride and Baratto.

Many young men entered the field of officiating but only a few made it all the way to the state finals. Some did not get there because of politics. Some did not get there because of weight. Some did not get there because they were not good enough. But Walt McFatridge may have had the best reason.

"Walt won the IHSAA Medal, now the Trester Award," said Bob Spay, "and was a darn good referee. He worked games for twelve years and had reached the regional level, well in line for a semistate. After his twelfth year had finished, he walked into the main office of the company where he worked in Kokomo in answer to a summons from his boss. "Walt, I am of the opinion you should be giving up this officiating thing as we pay you enough you should not have to referee."

Without hesitation, Walt answered, "Oh sir, I have already quit."

"Is that right? I didn't know."

"Yes sir."

"When did you give it up."

Walt grinned and said, "Sir, as of this moment!"

Do coaches respect a referee who calls a good game? "Yes," said Spay, "I believe they do. However, only a handful come close to what Columbus Coach Bill Stearman did after the 1960 Indianapolis semistate."

Spay tells the story: "Columbus was undefeated going into the game, and Muncie Central had lost only one game. It was one of those perfectly played ballgames from start to finish, and in the end, Columbus lost in a squeaker.

"We finished getting dressed and headed out the door. Now this was some twenty minutes after the game had ended. There, at the top of the stairs, stood every member of the defeated Columbus team. As we reached them, they were in a line, and each shook hands with us and congratulated us on an excellent refereed game. On the tail end of that row was Coach Stearman.

"I must admit," Spay said, "it was one of the great moments of my officiating life."

One other game stands out in Spay's long career. It was the final state tourney game in 1964.

"Two excellent teams, Huntington and Lafayette Jeff, battled it out for the championship. Jeff slipped ahead in the final minute and won, 58-55. During the game, Dick Jacobs and I called a total of twenty-three personal fouls, thirteen on Jeff and ten on Huntington.

"After the game was over and the awards presented, a reporter for the Huntington newspaper ask Huntington forward and Trester Award winner Mike Weaver about the officiating.

" 'If there were any mistakes in this game tonight,' said Weaver, 'they were made by the players, not the officials.' "

Young coaches learned early never to approach a referee prior to a game with any more than a casual greeting.

Del Harris, now a professional coach, was in his first year at Dale High School and they were facing a tough Evansville Lincoln ball club. Before the game started, Harris came over to Lowell Smith and Kenneth Blankenbaker and asked, "Fellas, how are you going to call them?"

"What do you mean?" Smith questioned.

"Well," asked Harris, "are you going to call them close or are you going to let the teams play?"

Smith, like a father teaching his son, said, "Coach, when this game is about two minutes old you will have to make up your own mind how we are calling them."

Lincoln walked all over Dale but Smith had made a friend, for he worked for Harris several times after that.

Smith refereed with Blankenbaker many times through the years, but his initial trip from Palmyra to Evansville in his partner's Volkswagen Bug was a one-time nightmare.

Rosie Holds An Unbeatable Record

Rosie Leedy holds a record that may never be broken in Indiana basketball. In 1976, her first year as a referee, she joined Lowell Smith in working the initial championship game of the Girls Tournament at Hinkle Fieldhouse, won by Warsaw over Bloomfield, 57-52. No male official has come close to moving up that quickly. Talk to her partner in the game, and you find he has nothing but high praise for her work.

Rosie credits the fact she knew basketball inside out because her husband is a coach, and that she not only worked a full schedule of girls games that first year, she also worked three boys games. She laughs while talking about the boys games, saying, "I never had to chase a loose ball and when I said something to a player, the answer always came back, 'Yes, m'am.' "

Her most embarrassing moment also came during a boys game. "The game was at Pioneer and when I checked with the coach for the number and name of his captain, he gave me the number and said the boys name was Stead. Since I did not want to interfere with the team practicing, I walked to the center of the floor, spotted the number under the basket and yelled, 'Hey Stud!'

"I am not sure who had the redder face, the team captain or me."

Pat Roy, IHSAA assistant commissioner, praised Rosie for her mechanics on the floor. "She was dramatic in her moves," said Roy, "and I well remember one out of bounds play in the state tournament when Rosie did a 360-degree whirl in giving the signal. There was never a doubt about her calls."

The final game holds several memories for Rosie: "I was thirty-seven years old and as I bent down to put the ball on the floor for the National Anthem, my knees cracked so loud Lowell heard them and we both laughed . . . the uneasy feeling of realizing a police corridor for us to exit at the end of the game meant this was serious business . . . the feeling of being in a vacuum when the bleacher lights were lowered and the crowd roared . . . and the emotion of the Warsaw girls when they knew they had the title won."

"I am 6'-2"," said Smith, "and Kenney is 5'-9" on his tiptoes. As soon as I got in the car I realized I was in trouble. My knees were crammed against the dash and my head hit the roof if I sat up straight. By the time we reached Evansville, it took a can opener to get me out of that Bug.

"Also," he continued, "it was below zero outside and that little manifold heater put out as much heat as a cigarette lighter.

"We got dressed and walked to the floor. My legs were so sore I could not run. I told Kenney he would have to call both ends for a few minutes until I worked out the cramps. It was a full five minutes before I was moving without pain.

"As he delivered me home I told him, never again. He either came in a different car next time or forget it.

"The next game we had together," laughed Smith, "Kenny came driving up in a new Fairlane Ford."

On two occasions in the seventies, Smith said a technical foul call turned games totally around and he has wondered since if he made the right decision.

"In the New Castle regional, Muncie Central was playing Shenandoah and Ray Pavy's team had a ten-point lead on the Bearcats with five minutes left in the final quarter. Berlin Rowe was the Muncie coach. There were nine thousand fans in that fieldhouse and seven thousand were rooting for Shenandoah.

"I called a foul on a Muncie player and Rowe came storming off the bench, protesting at the top of his voice. When he knew I could hear him he yelled, 'Call them the same at both ends of the floor.'

"I walked over to him, crossed my right hand flat over my left fingers and said, 'I will do just that.'

"We walked to the other end of the floor with the Muncie fans booing loud and long and the Shenandoah shooter missed two free throws, the technical shot and after taking the ball out of bounds, lost it to Muncie.

"Central proceeded to score eleven straight points and

won the game. A week later I received a letter from a Shenandoah fan telling me how good I was for three quarters and how lousy I was for one quarter. There is no doubt the tech call made the difference."

The second game where the technical changed the outcome was at Jennings County against Charlestown. Charlestown, coached by Scotty Daugherty, looked terrible throughout the first half, although on paper they had the better team.

In the third quarter, Ham Werneke, Jennings County coach, had his team rolling again, keeping Charlestown off balance. Then the pivotal play.

"It was a simple out-of-bounds play," said Smith, "but it went against Charlestown. As I took the ball and started to hand it to a Jennings County player, I realized Daugherty had raced down the entire length of the floor and was standing beside me yelling like an Apache."

"What kind of a call was that?" screamed the coach. "That was a terrible call. You are blind."

Smith asked, "Scotty, what are you doing down here?"

"Lowell," screamed the coach, "you got to do better than that. Terrible!"

Smith said he turned to the scorers bench, signaled a technical and told Daugherty to get on the bench.

From that moment on Charlestown caught fire and won the game in the final twenty seconds.

In the dressing room after the game, Smith said there was a knock and in walked Daugherty.

"Lowell," he said with a grin, "I'm sorry I got down there with you, but I had to go somewhere. We needed a wake-up call."

Often a referee finds out his wife is the biggest critic in the crowd.

The game was at Winchester against rival Union City. McBride and Hilligoss had taken a young referee with them to break him in. Each worked half of the B-game with him and as the two teams readied to jump to start the second half, they lined up facing the wrong way. Neither referee caught it.

Down the floor came Winchester and scored on a lay-up. Union City immediately scored on a fast break, but before any more action could take place the scorer's bench called McBride over.

"Mac," said the official scorer, "they are going the wrong way."

McBride answered, "I know it. You know it. But no one else knows it, so let's play it this way the rest of the half." That is what they did and no one ever said a word about it to the referees.

However, as McBride walked over to signal a foul near the end of the game, back of the bench sat his wife Reba, and Hilligoss' wife Sally . . . holding their noses.

Lowell Smith also had wife troubles. The game was at Marion and it was a "barn burner" until the final second when Elkhart missed its last shot and the host school won by one point.

Smith and his wife Gloria had barely cleared the Marion city limits when this conversation took place.

"Lowell," said his wife, "that charge-block call against Marion in the fourth quarter was the worst call I have ever seen you make."

"What!" countered the referee. "I was right. You were sitting in the Marion section and naturally, they are not going to agree with the call."

"No," stubbornly said his wife, "it was a lousy call."

That did it. For the next one hundred miles not one word was said by either husband or wife.

They were nearing the outskirts of Columbus when Gloria saw a mule by the side of the road.

"Is he any relation to you?" she asked her husband.

"Yes," answered the referee, "by marriage."

Smith got into trouble with his wife another time and he never did make her believe his explanation.

"She always packed my suitcase, knowing how meticulous I am about having everything in place and in dressing exactly the same each time.

"It turned out to be an excellent evening and Charlie Fouty and I worked a good game between Southridge and Huntingburg. After the game I showered and started to dress only to discover I did not have a fresh pair of shorts.

"Darn," Smith said to Fouty. "Gloria forgot to pack a clean pair of shorts."

"Hey, friend," said Fouty, "no problem. I always carry an extra pair. Here, put these on."

The Terre Haute referee handed Smith a pair of boxer shorts that had red roosters imprinted all over them. With trepidation, Smith put them on and headed home.

"As I walked into the bedroom," said Smith, "Gloria raised up and asked about the game. That is, she asked about the game until I unveiled my red-rooster shorts. 'What in the world is that?' she yelled, pointing at my shorts. Before I could say a word, she again yelled, 'Where did you get those things?'

"I tried to explain," said the referee, "but it was three days before she would even speak to me.

"The bad part was," said Smith, "I could hear Fouty laughing all the way from Terre Haute."

Smith came within an inch of losing an eye in a freak accident during the Princeton game at Tell City.

There was a capacity crowd on hand for the bitter rivalry between the two schools, so the officials agreed that the gun would sound to end a quarter, not the horn. With all the noise, the horn was not loud enough to be heard on the floor.

"I made one final statement before we tossed up the first jump," said Smith. "No matter what happened, the gun must sound to end a quarter. The horn meant nothing. All agreed.

"I glanced at the clock and saw there were only seconds left in the first quarter, but when the timer raised the gun and pulled the trigger, nothing happened. He pulled it twice more before it went off, maybe three or four seconds late. The problem was, in those few seconds, a Princeton player shot and hit and I signaled it good.

"At the bench the timer informed me that the buzzer had sounded before the shot and that the gun misfired. I told him the agreement was the gun must sound and the shot counted.

"The timer was fooling with the gun as I stood there, and suddenly it went off and the wad of the blank struck me an inch above the eye as well as scorching my neck and face. Dr. Ress, whom I had called upon in an earlier game when a wasp had stung me, came hurrying to the scorer's bench.

"He told me I was a fortunate man since the blank wad had come so close to my eye, but missed. I agreed. He patched me up and I finished the game.

"As for the gun, it worked perfectly the final three quarters."

Smith has the distinction of being the only Indiana male referee to be selected to appear in the National Federation of High School Athletic Association film, "Basketball Today." The movie was shot at Elgin, Illinois, in 1973, and distributed nationwide.

The National Federation makes the rules for basketball used in not only the United States, but also Canada, Guam and Puerto Rico. Each state was ask to submit one name for the filming and Indiana Commissioner Phil Eskew chose Smith. The second referee chosen was Mike Retica of Forest Lake, Illinois.

"It was a great experience," said the southern Indiana farmer. "It is especially interesting to me now seeing how I looked some twenty years ago. I sure would hate to try and get up and down the floor today like I did in that film. But if anyone questions me, I've got proof that I could do it with ease back then."

Smith was a master at handling any situation, one big

reason he was chosen, and his solutions even got a laugh from a coach on occasion.

"Scottsburg was playing Austin," said Smith, "and McKee Munk was handling the game with me. I was under the basket at the east end of the floor when a Scottsburg player shot, was closely guarded but not fouled, and missed. Austin got the rebound.

"Up the floor they came on a fast break and I saw a Scottsburg boy reach in so I whistled a foul.

"Jim Barley, the Scottsburg coach, came roaring off the bench, wanting a personal foul on Austin.

"Oh, Lowell," screamed Barley, "Pate pushed my boy. How could you miss that?"

"Who in the world is Pate?" Smith asked.

"He's that fuzzy headed, little guard from Austin," said Barley, "and he pushed off when he went past the head of the circle. You couldn't have missed seeing it."

Smith put his hand on the coach's shoulder and said, "Jim, I know just what you mean. When I came down the far side of the floor I thought I was going to sneeze and when you sneeze, you always shut your eyes and I probably did miss it."

There was a long pause, then Barley shook his head, grinned and said, "I'll know never to ask you about a play again."

3
Don't Fool With a Referee

Coaches throughout Indiana learned early in their careers that you must do everything you can to keep a referee satisfied, at least prior to a game. Jennings County Coach Don Jennings found this out in an early seventies game with Seymour and Don Snedeker was the referee.

It all started when the mercury dropped well below zero but when Snedeker and his wife left for the Jennings County gymnasium, there was no snow on the ground in Fayette County. By the time they reached the Rush County line, snow started piling up and within five miles it was two feet deep.

"We could not go more than twenty-five miles an hour," said the referee, "and I told my wife we were going to be close on time."

At North Vernon a bank sign registered fifteen below zero, and as Snedeker turned toward the high school on U.S. 50, all he could see in front of him were taillights. Traffic was solid and moving at a snail's pace. The referee glanced at his watch and saw they had almost an hour and a half until the eight o'clock game-time hour.

At 7:10, he turned into the school parking lot, gave a sigh of relief and rolled down his window to tell the policeman at the gate he was one of the referees and needed to park by the gymnasium entrance.

The policeman looked at him and said, "I don't care who you are, you have to park at the football field. This lot is full."

Snedeker could not believe his ears. "Maybe you didn't understand," he said, "I am one of the referees and I have a suitcase and garment bag to carry in for the game. I am not going to park a quarter mile away and carry this stuff."

"Mister," said the policeman, "maybe you didn't understand. This parking lot is full and you *will* park at the football field."

Now the referee was furious. "Look, whoever you are," yelled Snedeker, "you tell the school athletic director that Don Snedeker from Connersville was here to referee the game and that due to your stupidity, he went home."

Snedeker slammed the car in reverse and started backing out of the gate when he heard a thumping noise on his driver's side window. He stopped and realized the Jennings County sheriff was standing there, a man he knew.

"Hey Don," he asked, when the official rolled down his window, "where are you going?"

"I'm going home."

"You can't go home, you got a game to referee. This is the biggest game of the year."

"I couldn't care less. That cop up there at the gate told me I can't park by the gymnasium and I am not going to carry all this stuff through two feet of snow to referee a ballgame. Besides, my wife has on high heels so we can go on to a party at Rushville after the game. So, good-bye."

"Oh my God," moaned the sheriff. "Look, follow me and I'll take care of it."

The sheriff hurried to where the policeman was standing and Snedeker rolled his car slowly forward. He glanced at his watch and it showed 7:35. The sheriff said something to the policeman and he shrugged his shoulders.

"Get in there and park right next to the door," yelled the sheriff.

With a glare at the policeman, Snedeker did as the sheriff had instructed. As he got out of the car, Athletic Director Ham Werneke came running out.

"Where in the world have you been?" he asked. "We called the State Police to see if you had been in a wreck."

"I've been out there at the gate arguing with that damn cop for the past half hour. He refused to let me in even though I explained I needed to park close so I could carry my clothes and suitcase. I almost went home."

"I don't believe this," Werneke said.

"If it hadn't been for your sheriff," said the referee, "I would have been long gone."

The second referee, Roger McGriff, was waiting in the dressing room, and since Shelbyville had a half foot of snow on the ground by late afternoon, he had left early and arrived well ahead of time. "I'll get the prelims out of the way," he said, "while you get dressed."

Werneke walked to the floor with Snedeker, and as they neared the entrance, the referee said, "My wife better not be seated in peanut heaven or I may leave yet."

"Oh no, no," said the athletic director, "there she is in the third row VIP section."

The game started and with only three minutes gone, McGriff called a foul on a Jennings County player and the coach came bouncing off the bench in protest. Without a moment's hesitation, Snedeker, who was still furious, slapped him with a technical. The coach stopped in his tracks and did not say another word.

Snedeker went to Seymour Coach Barney Scott and ask for a shooter. They could hardly hear each other for the packed crowd booing the tech at the top of their lungs. The referee glanced toward the Jennings County bench as he took the ball and saw the coach lean over to the athletic director and say something. The shooter walked to the line and as the referee handed him the ball he said, "We sure are popular, aren't we?"

"Yeh," said Snedeker, "and son, if you ever made two free throws in your life, you make these two, 'cause I want them to hurt."

The official said the player grinned and said, "Give me that basketball." Both tosses were dead center.

At halftime, Werneke came to the dressing room with soft drinks and Snedeker asked, "Ham, what did your coach say to you when I called that technical?"

The AD laughed, "He said, you make damn sure he's got a place to park the next time he comes here to referee."

A few weeks later, Snedeker had the holiday tournament at Jennings County and when he drove up to the gate the policeman said, "Yes, sir, Mr. Snedeker, see that place right up there by the door? That's yours."

Winfield (Dick) Jacobs and his brother Danny found out you'd better use the right name or you can park in the far-distant lot like the rest of the fans.

Danny and Dick were to work a game at Princeton down in Gibson county, and it was the first time there for either referee. As they drove up to the gate a guard stopped them. Dick rolled down his window and asked, "Is this where the officials park?"

"No sir," said the man, "you gotta park over there in the big lot, this is reserved for the referees."

Battling snowstorms was common practice for referees who traveled the state to work games.

Joe Mullins and Charles (Pup) Garber were heading from Kokomo to Fort Wayne for the Fort Wayne sectional when snow started falling. It was light so Mullins, who was driving, did not worry about it. But after the night game, when the two referees walked out of the fieldhouse, snow was knee deep.

"We debated about staying in Fort Wayne, but decided we would give it a try since we had good roads home," said Mullins. "We got to Huntington without problems, other than visibility, and stopped at a restaurant to get some coffee. Everyone was talking about how bad it was, but soon we shoved off again.

"This time we made it to Peru, slowly and carefully, and again stopped at a diner for coffee. It actually was a

Why Would Anyone Want To Referee?

Why would any referee drive one hundred miles, sometimes in knee-deep snow, pavements glassy with ice, duck-drowning rains, London fogs or howling winds, often return well after midnight, take a beating of boos from a crowd and abuse from the coaches, all for a paycheck of $15? By the time any referee paid for a meal and bought the gasoline for his car, he lost money.

The answer? A love for the game of basketball.

"You do not get rich refereeing," said Don McBride, "although today the pay is better. A top official will get up to $50 per game now. I worked both the A and B games and often received $10 for the evening."

Even the referee 1995 handbook talks about it.

"For practically all basketball officials, officiating is an interesting hobby, a pleasant vocation and an opportunity to continue association and friendships in the world of sports. Ordinarily, it is not a way of earning a living. Anyone who becames a high school basketball official with the hope of thereby earning a livelihood is doomed to disappointment. The rewards will be in the nature of continuing athletic activity, of friendships gained, youth renewed and the satisfaction of having rendered an important service to the youth of the communities involved and to the game itself.

"A prospective official who is unwilling to devote many hours to this avocation had better give it up before starting. Intensive study is necessary. Included in the materials which one must master are the rules themselves, related study materials and the mechanics and techniques of officiating a game. While on the playing floor, the official is responsible to the IHSAA, the local official's group, the national rules committee and to each player on the two teams.

"When the game ends, your duties are over. Take a shower, dress, collect your gear and head for home. Never look back!"

big truck stop and I saw a rig head into the parking lot from the south. I cornered the driver when he walked in. "How is it south?" Mullins asked. "Horrible," answered the trucker. "That bad?" questioned the referee.

"Mister," said the trucker, "you ain't seen bad 'til you hit that road. If you plan to go that way, forget it. I don't think you can get through."

Mullins said the two referees again discussed staying in Peru, but decided they had gotten this far, so what the heck. Out they went.

"That drive from Peru south was as bad as the trucker had said," Mullins continued. "Time and time again I thought my car was stuck, only to somehow break out of it for a few more feet. Finally I made it to Pup's driveway and headed for my home."

Mullins lives in a small town outside Kokomo named Cassville, and it was a tremendous relief when he turned off U.S. 31 onto the Cassville road, less than a half mile to go. He barely made it around two sharp curves and to the turn left that led to his house.

"I could see the lights on in the house and they sure did look good after almost four hours on the road. I turned the corner, only a thousand feet to go, when suddenly snow flew up over the hood and my car came to a crushing stop. There I was, within sight of my house, mired so deep in a snow bank I had to work another ten minutes to get my door open so I could walk home.

"Never in my life," said Mullins, "have I been as happy to see a smiling wife waiting at the door as I was that night."

McBride and Hilligoss worked many games together and trusted each other to the letter while on the floor. But when it came to predicting the weather, McBride found out his partner was the senior official.

The phone rang and when Hilligoss picked it up, McBride said, "John, there is a big snowstorm coming. I think we should take the train up to Kokomo since we both have to be at work first thing in the morning." Hilligoss argued they could drive it, but McBride insisted and finally won out.

The trip up was great as they enjoyed the scenery along the tracks. A taxi delivered them to the gymnasium in plenty of time for the game. When it was over and the two referees walked outside the building, there was only the thinnest covering of snow. Hilligoss did not say a word as Kokomo Coach Joe Platt drove them to the depot. But when they checked the time the train was expected, the clerk informed them it would be 3:30 a.m.

The two referees looked at the short, hard benches, shrugged their shoulders and tried to stretch out as best they could. But neither got any sleep and only dozed when they finally boarded the train.

It was 6:30 a.m. when the train reached Richmond and the street lights of the city revealed absolutely no snow on the ground whatsoever. They ate a quick bite at the depot restaurant and headed for work. At this point, Hilligoss had to get in one last word. "You and your ideas," he hollered at McBride as the latter crawled into his car.

Getting to and from a game in a snowstorm was not unusual. But staying overnight in a gymnasium when the snow was too deep to leave, is another story. Oddly enough, these deep snows seemed to always happen at sectional or regional time.

Howard Plough and Jim Davis had the 1961 sectional at Whiteland, near Greenwood. The men worked the games through Friday evening without problems, spending the night in a nearby motel in order to be there for the Saturday semifinals and the championship game.

"When we looked out the motel window on Saturday morning," said Plough, "the snow had blanketed our car until you could not recognize it. We knew we were in trouble.

"So, we hurriedly got dressed, shoved the snow off the car, drove to a restaurant to eat breakfast, and then headed to the gymnasium. By game time the snow was four feet deep and coming down in buckets full. The man handling the sectional announcements ask for the crowd's attention some fifteen minutes before the opening toss. He told them that if anyone in the gym wanted to make it home, he or she better get started now. Very few left.

"At that moment," said the referee, "all power failed in the building, the lights went out and the heat went off. It was eerie for a few seconds as 3,500 people became perfectly quiet. Then we heard shouts of play ball and after a quick consultation with tourney officials, we got underway.

"The light was all right to play," he continued, "but in a few minutes we realized it was getting colder and colder. We knew the temperature outside was in the teens, but we did not think about the gymnasium dropping that fast. By the end of the second game the people in the stands looked more like football fans than basketball fans. We were freezing on the floor but did not wear our warm-up jackets for fear they would slow us down.

"The afternoon session ended," Plough continued, "and there was no way anyone could leave the school, the snow was drifted shoulder high by this time. So, Jim and I joined 3,500 frigid people in sleeping in the gym, on the stage and in the dressing rooms. I never knew anything could be as dark as it was that night, after the last dim glow of light disappeared." Snowplows opened the roads and parking lot by noon on Sunday and people attempted to get home. The tournament's final game was played on Monday night to brilliant lights and warm conditions.

It was not snow that created an unusual situation for Plough on another occasion. It was a faulty scoreboard that went totally blank. Referees often wondered why these malfuctions always seemed to happen in a crucial game. "The Noblesville tournament had been a good one, but as expected, the host team had rolled over its opponents until the final game," recalled Plough. "Early in the third quarter, and with the score tied, the scoreboard, including the clock, stopped working.

"We halted the game and every trick of the trade was used to get it going, but to no avail. The only answer was to keep score on a blackboard at one end of the gymnasium, keep the time on a stopwatch, and every thirty seconds have the announcer give the time left.

"Somehow we got through it without a major incident," Plough said, "but I never wanted to go through something like that again."

A faulty clock caused official Bill May to have some uneasy moments, and to this day he is not positive he made the right call. This happened in the Lawrenceburg sectional in 1966.

The final game had Coach Bud Bateman's excellent Lawrenceburg team against Aurora. Coach Carl Hughes knew the only hope his team had against Lawrenceburg was to play a control game, and they did.

Lawrenceburg got an early lead and appeared headed for an easy win. But slowly Aurora came back and with a minute to go in the game, the score was tied . . . big upset in the making.

Bateman called time out and told his players to hold the ball for one last shot. With ten seconds to go a Lawrenceburg player forgot the closely guarding rule and May called a held ball. May tossed the ball up for the jump, and the Aurora center tipped it to Aurora's excellent guard Mike McCarter.

"The problem was," said May, "McCarter had an unusual move when he started to dribble and sometimes he traveled and sometimes he did not. He got the tip at the sideline and did a toe dance to keep from going out of bounds, but no travel. He then saw the big center, Kuhlmeier, open and shot a pass to him. Kuhlmeier spun, fired, hit and was fouled.

"I looked at the clock," May continued, "and it showed three seconds left. If Kuhlmeier made his shot, it was over, since the three-point rule was not known in those days.

But he missed and the ball bounced to the right where Lawrenceburg grabbed it and signalled time out.

"Again I looked at the clock and it showed three zeros, time expired. I hurried to the timer, for I had not heard the buzzer, but in the roar of the crowd I could have missed it."

Enter a new factor. Jake Senitza was a senior on Lawrenceburg and was far from being the best player on the team. But in this outing he had played the game of his life, only to lose in the final seconds. His father was the official timer.

"I checked with the other official, Bob Wells, and he thought it had sounded, but could not be positive. So we turned to Senitza for the answer and he admitted he was so involved in the final play he could not give us a truthful yes or no."

Naturally the Lawrenceburg coach was screaming it did not sound and Hughes was screaming just as loud that it was over. As the senior official it was up to May to make the call.

He turned from the bench, the crowd quieted and he announced, "The clock shows three zeroes . . . the game is over."

In the dressing room May was relieved to have a local sports writer say he heard the buzzer.

"But," said May, "I should have had the timer turn on the clock to see if it would sound the buzzer, or if it already had sounded. Hindsight is better than foresight."

It was the Fort Wayne Sectional, held at the coliseum, and Gene Butts was working with Warsaw's Frank Sanders in the final game. Fort Wayne Southside was favored to win, but Fort Wayne Central Catholic had other ideas and the game was nip and tuck throughout.

There was one problem at the coliseum, later corrected. The timer sat off the level of the floor and when the crowd would leap to its feet, he could not see the corners.

The score was tied and Catholic had the ball. A player in the corner signalled time-out and immediately Sanders called it. But the timer did not see the signal. Since the Catholic player had seen Sanders signal time-out, he dropped the ball. A Southside player grabbed it and scored just as the buzzer sounded to end the game.

The Southside crowd went wild, but here was Sanders running toward the scorer's bench waving his arms. He told the timer he had signaled time out with six seconds to play and that the Southside basket did not count. The ball belonged to Catholic.

Confusion reigned as Southside Coach Don Reichert rushed to the bench. Sanders explained what had happened, but Reichert would not accept his explanation. The referee did not want to call a technical on the coach, for it was a confused issue and the fault of the facility and not the timer or referees.

Finally calm was restored and the game resumed with the clock set at six seconds. Central Catholic did get one shot off before regulation time ended, but it missed and the game was settled in overtime.

There are times when a referee pins a technical on one coach, only later to learn he missed one on the other end.

"But," said Sanders, "when the game has been over for a couple hours, there is little you can do about it."

It was the 1960 state final game between the Muncie Central Bearcats and East Chicago. Midway through the third quarter, Central Coach John Longfellow charged onto the floor after a call and Sanders whistled a technical on him.

"Sure," screamed Longfellow, "I get a T for protesting a bad call and you let Baratto (Coach Johnnie Baratto) get by with murder."

"John," said the referee, "I haven't seen Baratto do anything wrong. Now go sit down while we shoot this technical."

That night Sanders was watching the ten o'clock news in his hotel room when highlights of the Muncie-East Chicago game were shown. Only moments before Longfellow caught his T, the camera showed Baratto ripping off his sport coat after a call and throwing it into the crowd. Sanders, to an empty room, said, "John, I take it all back."

It never hurts for a young official to have a good outing with a veteran, especially in a close, hard-fought contest. Coach Art Beckner's Muncie Central Bearcats and Coach Ralph Holmes' Bedford Stonecutters were well matched before Beckner suspended his star center for an infraction that one game.

Dee Williams was hired to work with McBride, and it was the first time they had worked together.

"We were no more than two minutes into the game when I knew I had a sharp young man on the other side of the floor," said McBride. "He was on top of every play, moved into position flawlessly and made his calls with authority."

The game was as close as billed and Muncie, which was picked to win the state that year, lost to Bedford by one point.

After the game McBride told Williams, "Dee, you got a good whistle. You hang tight like that and you are going to be all right."

A few days later McBride saw Commissioner Phillips and told him, "I worked with a very good official in the game between Muncie and Bedford."

"Who?"

"Dee Williams from Brazil."

"I'll check into it." Phillips did and Williams moved quickly in the tournament ranks.

Early in his career, Don Snedeker saw the antics of McBride and often patterned some of his calls after the senior official. This was not unusual as the IHSAA suggested that B-team referees stick around for the A-game and take mental notes.

"McBride and Hilligoss were working the A-game after I had teamed up with another rookie to work the B-game at Connersville. We had seats by the official bench since it was wise to stay for the main game. Some five rows up, directly back of us, sat a beautiful blonde woman and from the opening whistle she was on McBride like jelly on a roll. He took her ranting the entire first half without a word.

"The third quarter was less than a minute old when Don called a charging foul right in front of this young woman. She leaped to her feet, jumped up and down and screamed, 'McBride, I would like to see you after this game.' McBride turned to her, and you could have heard a pin drop as he yelled back, 'Honey, any time, any place . . . I'll be there.'

"We never heard another peep out of her the rest of the way."

In days now long past, referees were reluctant to say anything to a woman fan, simply because it was not proper to do so. But there were times when an official reached his wit's end, and Dee Williams got there in a game at Indianapolis Tech.

Play had barely started when a woman six rows up was on Williams on every call. Everything he whistled was wrong, and she could be heard far and wide as she screamed at him.

At the end of the first quarter, the second referee wondered to Dee what he planned to do? In a close game her screaming could stir up a crowd to frenzy and they could not allow that to happen.

"I'll take care of it," said the senior official. Early in the second quarter, Williams called a moving violation right in front of where the woman was seated, and she leaped to her feet and could be heard in the next county.

Williams blew his whistle to stop action, walked over to the woman and said, "Lady, I have never kicked a woman out of a gymnasium in my fifteen years as a referee, but you are about to become the first."

"Pure silence until the final gun," laughed Williams.

There is no doubt one woman fan, screaming at the referees with a high pitched voice, could be heard on the floor above the roar of five thousand other rooters. When it came to this, Marge Kennett of Rushville was in a class by herself.

McBride and Hilligoss were heading from the dressing room to the gym floor for the Connersville at Rushville game when McBride said, "I wonder if my biggest critic, Marge Kennett, will be here tonight?"

When they reached the floor, sure enough, there was Marge and next to her sat a Catholic priest. So, McBride walked over, sat down next to the priest and said, "Father, would you try and contain this young woman here? She really gets carried away."

Before the priest could answer, Marge yelled, "Me! Me! Just wait, McBride, you haven't seen anything yet." She leaned over and pointed to the priest, "He's even worse than I am and there is no one here to contain him."

McBride looked at Marge and the smiling priest, grinned and said, "Enjoy yourselves."

Even the wives of the coaches got into the act. For McBride, Barney Scott's wife Marguerite, down at Seymour, was a prime critic. Since she knew the referee on a first-name basis, she did not hesitate to let him know when she thought a call was wrong.

Seymour was in a close game when McBride called a traveling violation on a Seymour player, nullifying his field goal. As he went down the floor, Marguerite yelled from the bleachers, "You blew it Mac. Bad call."

On his next trip past her seat the referee yelled back, "Marguerite, you know I called it right. Now sit there and be quiet."

McBride said she grinned at him and continued to let him have it on any call on which she disagreed.

Danny Jacobs also had woman problems, but his started before the game.

Jacobs was working with Bill Hile at Sandborn in Knox

County. It was a small school and the referees were forced to dress in the same room where men were popping popcorn in an old-fashioned popper.

"Bill and I had just reached the buff degree and were reaching for our jock straps, when in walked a woman. We grabbed for our pants to cover up and I knocked over my chair in doing so. One of the men turned toward us and casually said, 'Hey fellows, don't worry about it . . . it's just my wife.'

"I must admit," said Jacobs, "it made Bill and me feel like inanimate objects and we began to wonder if that was the general outlook basketball fans had of referees."

Officials must be on their guard all the time for fear a fan or school official believes they are being too friendly with an opposing coach, principal, superintendent or even other fans.

Don Snedeker was officiating the second game of the Washington regional and it was a case of three big school teams against one small school. Jasper had the powerhouse but the small school had a 5-6 player who could shoot the eye out of a potato.

The official decided to dress and go watch the first game and was joined by Jimmy Dimitroff, the second referee. Snedeker had no more than seated himself in a chair by the official bench when Jasper Athletic Director Don Nobblett came walking up. The referee had worked several games for Nobblett when he was coach at Parker in Randolph County and they had not seen each other for ten years.

The two men shook hands and chatted for a half minute or so, smacked each other on the shoulder as a farewell, and Snedeker sat back down.

The small school won its afternoon game and the hotshot shooter scored thirty-four points. Jasper also won, setting up an evening match between the two. Snedeker had the game.

"It was no match," said the referee. "The huge Jasper

team overpowered its opponent and the small school star was totally stopped by Jasper's 6'-6" center. He scored less than ten points.

"The next week I got my semistate assignment for Lafayette and after dressing, decided to watch a few minutes of the first game before working game No. 2. At the end of the first quarter I decided to go to the dressing room and relax in a comfortable chair. As I stood up, IHSAA Commissioner Phil Eskew leaned over to me and said, 'We've got to talk.'

"In the dressing room," Snedeker continued, "Eskew started quizzing me."

"You ever been to Jasper before last week?"

"Not for a long time."

"Do you have any relatives living in Jasper?"

"No, none."

"Do you know anyone living in Jasper?"

"No, only the coach and the athletic director. Why?"

"Oh, it was the athletic director you were talking to a week ago at the regional?"

"Sure. I knew Don when he coached at Parker. I worked several games for him. Oh, now I know where you are coming from. We shook hands before the first game and talked maybe thirty seconds or so. What's up?"

"I had a mother call me," said the commissioner, "and she said Don was your brother-in-law and you should be barred from working any Jasper games. I told her I didn't believe it but would check it out."

The woman who called was the mother of the shooter who was stopped cold by the 6'-6" Jasper center.

Referees hate to see a game end on a free throw. But a friendly pat by McBride, in the last second, sent a wrong picture to the press.

The sectional final between Indianapolis Tech and Southport had been close all the way. A Tech player rolled under for a shot and Hilligoss whistled a foul on Southport. Since you could not see the clock from the floor at Butler

Fieldhouse, McBride went to the bench to check on how much time was left. "One second," answered the timer, "and Southport is ahead by one."

As McBride went back to the foul line he tossed the ball to Hilligoss and headed toward the out-of-bounds line. When he passed the shooter he patted the young man on the rear and said, "One second to play."

The Tech player hit both free throws and Southport lost by one point.

What McBride did not know was, a photographer for the *Indianapolis Star* shot a picture just as McBride patted the Tech player. The next day it appeared in the paper with a caption that said, "One official was so bad, he patted the shooter to give him confidence."

Jewell Young, the Southport coach, never forgave McBride and the Richmond official learned a valuable lesson . . . never touch a player.

The exact opposite happened at New Castle when a friendly hand from McBride quieted the crowd.

Muncie Central was playing the Trojans in the old Church Street gymnasium and it was packed to the rafters. From the opening tip-off the crowd was on McBride. New Castle had the No. 1 team in the state and Central got off to a fast start. Whalen, one of New Castle's star players, along with Ellis and Wright, was fouled hard and went tumbling to the floor. The partisan crowd leaped to its feet in unison and booed loud and long.

McBride turned away from signaling the scorer's bench and started trotting toward the other end foul line. When he got to Whalen, the big center was sitting, trying to recover from the foul. McBride reached down and lifted him to his feet, not an easy task since Whalen weighed in at over two hundred pounds.

The move by the referee totally silenced the crowd. You could have heard a pin drop. Whalen looked at the referee and said loud enough for everyone to hear, "Mr. McBride, we sure shut them up didn't we."

The New Castle coach later said Whalen could not get over McBride's lifting him to his feet.

Anyone who thinks officials are not up to any situation should have been with Don Snedeker, Bluffton Coach Jack Cross and referees Charlie Stump, Carl Fleetwood and Jim Ladd at Indianapolis, in a pouring rain. Let Snedeker tell it:

"We had been out to eat the night before the state finals and were headed west on 38th Street, going back to our hotel on Meridian. But when we got to the turn for Meridian the traffic was solid and every time we got the green light some car would have the other lane blocked and we couldn't move. We must have sat there a good ten minutes.

"Suddenly I heard the back door of my car open and Charlie Stump say, 'I'll take care of this.' The next thing I knew, there was Charlie in the glare of my headlights, signaling traffic in the other lane to stop. He actually walked right in front of the cars and held up his arms.

"Seeing an opening, I quickly made the turn and as I passed Charlie I again heard my back door open. As he jumped in he yelled, 'Piece of cake! Let's go.' The nut could have been killed."

Older referees often tried to con their younger partners into carrying their suitcases or being the designated driver or being responsible for going after all loose balls and on and on. Seldom did it work, but when it did, it took an elaborate plan to pull it off.

Snedeker was to work the first game of the Jefferson County Tournament in Madison with Bob Beeson. He had tried several times to get Beeson to carry his suitcase, since they often worked games together.

"Homer Owens and I drove to Madison to meet the other referees for breakfast," said Snedeker. "Beeson was standing outside the front door as I drove up. So, when I got out of the car I started limping."

"What happened to you?" he asked.

"I sprained my ankle feeding the hogs this morning and I don't know whether I can make it or not."

"Here," said Beeson, hurrying down the steps, "let me help you."

He took Snedeker's arm and helped him in the door and to the table where the other referee, Bill Graham, was waiting. Beeson fussed over Snedeker all during the meal, asking a half dozen times, "Do you think you can work?" He always got a painful, "I don't know."

Beeson drove and Snedeker rode with him to the gymnasium. When he crawled out of the car, Snedeker hobbled to the rear as Beeson opened the trunk.

"Wait, Don," said Beeson, "let me get that suitcase for you."

As the four referees entered the gym, Owens got into the act by helping Snedeker along.

While they were dressing, Beeson said, "Look Don, I'll cover the ends and you stay out. I'll get all the loose balls. You take it easy. We got to get you through this."

After the prelims were finished and Snedeker had whispered to both coaches what he was doing, he hobbled to the center of the floor for the opening jump. The ball went into the air and was tipped long toward the Southwestern goal. Snedeker took off like a shot, cutting to the sideline and under the basket, the position he would normally take.

Those watching Beeson said the referee's eyes got as big as silver dollars. He froze right in the middle of the floor and the whistle fell out of his mouth.

"During, after and for a long time," laughed Snedeker, "he called me every name under the sun.

"Oh yes," he added, "I thanked him for finally carrying my suitcase. His answer is unprintable."

Cy Birge may have pulled the ultimate con on a group of referees, but he denies he had anything to do with it.

McBride, Hilligoss, Homer Owens and Wes Oler were assigned to the Evansville semistate in 1959, so they left Richmond Friday noon to be ready for Saturday. Also, it gave them a chance to stop and visit with referee friends along the way, generally meeting at a local watering hole. Since they did not want to eat at every stop, they would order a drink and sip on it while gabbing together. Only McBride, who was driving, drank Cokes.

By the time they reached Jasper they had stopped three times, sipped three times and now met Birge for one last stop before Evansville. They spent an hour with him, still sipping, and then headed west.

"I was being extremely careful to obey the traffic lights and the speed limit," said McBride, "for even a hint of liquor in the car could have caused big trouble with the IHSAA. Suddenly, to my dismay, I saw the red lights of a crusier back of me and I must admit, I had a cold chill go up my back."

"Did you realize you went through a light back there on caution?" asked the deputy.

"No, officer," said McBride, rolling his window down only a fourth of the way.

"Well you did," the officer continued. "You Wayne County people think you can come to our part of the state and do anything you want to. I ought to run you in."

"I'll be careful and make sure it doesn't happen again," answered the referee.

The deputy leaned over and looked at the other three in the car and then said, "All right, I'll let you go this time. Just take it easy."

To this day, McBride believes Birge set the entire thing up, having a deputy friend stop the referees simply to give them a good scare. Whether he did or not, the end result was one the Richmond official never forgot.

Referee Odie Barnett makes sure no one is injured as a player goes into the crowd at Civic Hall in Richmond, chasing a loose ball.
-Richmond Palladium-Item *photo*

*Referee Gene Butts leaves no doubt as he whistles a foul in this 1969
regional game at New Castle.*
-Richmond Palladium-Item *photo*

*Referee Wayne Hinchman signals a ball out of bounds to the white
team in this 1968 action. Each referee had his own classic style of
indicating infractions.*
-Richmond Palladium-Item *photo*

The opening tip signaled the beginning of another high school basketball battle. Referee Cliff Dickman does the honors in this sixties game at Centerville.
    -Richmond Palladium-Item *photo*

Referees worked pre-season games to get in shape for the grinding schedule that lay ahead. In this 1969 Richmond workout, Referee Bill May signals a violation and leaves no doubt about the call.
    -Richmond Palladium-Item *photo*

This sign at the south end of Swayzee tells the story of the longest game in Indiana history. Referees Bill May and John Thomas worked the marathon game, won by Swayzee.
-Photo by Fritz Morgenstern

In this early sixties game at Williamsburg, Don McBride calls a contact violation on an attempted pass. When McBride whistled a foul, he not only indicated with distinct motions but you could hear the "you hacked" call throughout the gymnasium.
-Richmond Palladium-Item photo

76

4
Referees Enjoyed Their Day

Homer Owens, Jr., was an excellent referee, but he did take a lot of ribbing over his name. In basketball, a homer is a referee who gives the home team a clear advantage. Therein lies the kidding by other referees and coaches alike.

But when it came to making decisions on the court, there were few with more level heads than Owens.

Pat Malaska was coaching at Richmond, and in the heat of a game, often got carried away.

It was early in the third quarter when a Richmond guard stole the ball at mid-court, drove for the basket and used the rim to keep the opposing player from blocking his shot. Malaska leaped to his feet as the ball went in, and as the player headed down the floor, the coach ran onto the floor to smack his guard on the rear to congratulate him.

Owens came up and asked, "Pat, what are you doing out here on the floor."

Malaska looked around in wonderment and said, "Oh, my, how did I get out here."

Owens said he could have called a technical but saw no reason to do so. Malaska's being on the floor had not interfered with the game and Owens said he liked to see a coach show enthusiasm.

A similar incident happened to McBride when Malaska was then coaching at Peru. His team was playing at Fort Wayne Central and the host players scored three consecutive times on fast breaks. As McBride signaled the third basket and turned around, there was Malaska in the middle of the floor.

"What are you doing out here?" McBride asked.

"I'm guarding," answered Malaska, "no one else is."

McBride said, "Pat, get off the floor, now!"

The Peru coach grinned and sheepishly hurried to the bench. As McBride went past the Fort Wayne bench, Coach Herb Banet called out, "Mac, if that had been me, I would have gotten a technical."

McBride yelled back, "Herb, he's funny . . . you're not," and the game continued.

Some coaches, however, cannot take a referee's putting them in their place. Dick Baumgartner was one and Homer Owens got the best of the deal.

Baumgartner, an excellent coach, was at Crawfordsville, prior to taking the Richmond job, and in a regional game with Covington, Owens had to set the coach down on two occasions. Crawfordsville was getting beat and the coach blamed the referees. Owens warned Baumgartner to quiet down or he would put a T on him. That game resulted in a cool relationship between the coach and referee when Baumgartner went to Richmond.

While refereeing a game at New Castle, Owens heard from another official that Baumgartner was going to pay off the referee's contract and not have him for the last game of the season, Anderson at Richmond. However, he knew Owens had the Richmond game at Connersville, so he planned to keep the cancellation quiet until that game was over.

Owens tells the story this way:

"There was a rule that year that said the coach must be seated comfortably on the bench before play could resume. I made a call against Richmond that Baumgartner did not like, and he leaped to his feet only a short distance from me. I looked at him and he quickly sat down. But, in his rush to not get a technical, he sat too far back on the bench and over he went backwards, his feet straight up in the air.

"The Connersville crowd roared. I looked down at him

Ridiculous Rules

There have been several basketball rules through the years that Don McBride says were ridiculous. Here are a few he listed.

"In 1913 a rule said if the referee decreed a player was face guarding his opponent, it was a foul. It was a judgment call and a bad rule.

"In 1920 a new rule said a player could not reenter the game more than one time. This lasted until 1944, when unlimited substitution was adopted.

"In 1937 it was ruled that only two overtimes would be permitted and the game would then end in a tie. This lasted one year. Sudden death was introduced, whereby the first field goal scored in overtime resulted in a win. This terrible rule ended in 1961 when three minute, unlimited overtime periods were installed.

"The year 1943 saw another foolish rule when one free throw was to be given for each part of a double or multiple foul. In other words, if two players fouled one player, that one player got two free throws. I called it only one time and the Scottsburg Coach 'Whiskey' Seeler said, 'I never saw that in my life.'

I answered, 'Whiskey, you never had me refereeing before.' It was changed the next year.

"In 1983, long after I retired, the dumbest rule change in history went into the books. It was the adoption of the alternating possession rule for all jump or held balls. Let's say Richmond is playing Marion and as a Marion player shoots the ball is blocked and there is a scramble on the floor that results in a tieup. The referee looks at the alternating possession arrow and it points to Marion. So the Richmond defense is punished for making a good defensive play as the ball is given back to Marion. It simply does not make sense. Jumping the ball, as we did before 1983, is more fair than the present rule."

and politely inquired, 'are you all right, Dick?' He yelled back, 'Go ahead and play.' I answered as sweetly as possible, 'sorry, but you know the new rule says a coach must be comfortably seated on the bench before play resumes and you do not look very comfortable.' He glared at me and hurried around the end of the bench and back to his seat.

"I learned later that my wife was sitting in the crowd with IHSAA Commissioner Phil Eskew. When he saw the exchange between the coach and me, he leaned over to her, put his hand to his mouth and said, 'Homer is having a ball with Baumgartner.' He was right and I loved every moment of it," laughed the referee.

Owens started in 1943, worked three state finals and as of this writing, is the only father to have his son, Rick, also work the state championship. Rick has worked two, 1991 and 1995.

From the opening gun there was no doubt Homer Owens would be a good official, proving his merit in an unusual way.

His first game was at the Losantville Hall in Randolph County and pitted Modoc against Center of Delaware County. Gail Gaddis had the game with him. After the game ended the two referees were dressing when Mr. Keesling, the Center principal, came walking into the room.

"Mr. Owens," he asked, "do you have a week from today open? We have a home game and I would like to get you to call it."

"Let's see," said Owens. "Next Friday. I'll have to check my schedule and get back with you tomorrow. Is that okay?"

"Tomorrow will be fine," answered the principal. After he left, Gaddis started laughing.

"You lying sack," he said, "you don't have a game scheduled the rest of the year and you know it."

"Hey," replied Owens, "you wouldn't want him to think I'm a rookie would you?"

A no-call by a referee is as important as a call, if the situation merits it.

In the 1961 New Castle sectional the Trojans and Lewisville were locked in a tight game when, late in the third quarter, a Lewisville boy was injured. Lewisville had been leading by seven points at halftime, but New Castle had come back to trail by only three.

As Lewisville Coach Bob Scott came to see about the injury, instead of kneeling down as expected, he stopped beside Owens and asked, "Les Ray [Trojan coach] didn't get to you at the half, did he?"

Owens easily could have blown a technical at that point but since no one else heard the coach, and it was not going to affect the calls by the referee, he simply ignored the remark, walked around to the other side of the injured player and did not say a word. Scott kneeled down by his player and within a few minutes, action started again.

After the game was over and all the aftermath of winning a sectional had subsided, Scott came to see Owens. He said:

"Homer, you are a better man than I am. You easily could have put a technical on me, but you didn't."

"Bob, that was no time for a technical and I was in no position to give you one. No one else knew what happened and your remark did not influence me one bit."

Since that time, Owens and Scott have remained good friends. When Owens had his first chance to work with McBride, he was warned he would not get along with the veteran official because of McBride's showboating.

"That certainly did not prove true," said Owens. "Not only did I enjoy working with Mac, we had many games together through the years and not one cross word. In fact, Don helped me get my first sectional and I will always be grateful."

Owens got his first sectional in 1952, his first regional in 1956 and his first semistate five years later. By Friday evening of 1961, he had given up hope for a call when the telephone rang.

"I had just walked into the house from subbing as a school bus driver and hurried to answer the phone. It was Mr. Phillips."

"Mr. Owens," asked the commissioner, "what are you doing tomorrow?"

"Well, sir, I was planning on going to Indianapolis to watch the semistate."

"That's too bad," answered Phillips, "we wanted you to work the semistate at Fort Wayne."

Owens said he gulped and quickly answered, "Sir, I easily can change my plans."

He said he heard Phillips chuckle and then he said, "Have a good tournament."

Oddly enough, Owens was paired with Dick Jacobs and it also was Jacobs' first semistate. They called the Kokomo-Huntington game and Kokomo won the state that year. Huntington, a team loaded with freshmen, won it three years later when those freshmen were seniors.

Seldom is a referee assigned to a tournament game where a team from his semistate area is playing. This was not true in Owens' third semistate in 1964, The games were played at Indianapolis. When he got to Butler Fieldhouse he discovered he would work with Bob Spay on the Muncie Central-Columbus game.

Before the game the commissioner and his assistant came into the dressing room. After chatting a few minutes, they turned to leave and Phillips said, "Not to make you nervous, but whoever wins this game will win the state."

In unison the two referees said, "Thanks a lot!!"

He was right, Muncie Central defeated Columbus and the next week, won the state title.

"That semistate game was, beyond any doubt, the toughest game I ever refereed," said Owens. "One bad call against Columbus would have been devastating since I lived near Muncie."

After the game, Phillips returned to the dressing room, this time to congratulate the two referees on a good job.

"Sir," asked Owens, "why did you assign me to this game since I am from the Muncie semistate area?"

With a sly grin the commissioner said, "Mr. Owens, you handled it all right didn't you? That's why we had you here."

One final point, both Coaches Ike Tallman at Central, and Bill Stearman of Columbus, thought the game well officiated and in later years, used both referees several times.

Bob Showalter refereed for many years, not only Indiana high school games, but also in the Big 10. But this incident took place when he was the captain and star player of the Fountain City Little Giants in Wayne County.

Fountain City, coached by Cloyce Quakenbush, and Milton, with Bob Davis at the helm, were huge favorites in 1953 to meet in the final game of the Wayne County Tournament, and the winner was a toss-up. But both were upset in the afternoon semi-finals.

In the consolation game that night, Showalter came to the center of the floor as captain, looked around at the crowd and said to Owens, "Well, the right two teams are here. We are just an hour early."

Owens said he knew at that moment that this young man had a big future in sports, no matter what he decided to do. In later years he worked several games with Showalter, who is known as one of the best.

Coaches may earn a technical, only to come back with a remark later that nullifies any animosity. Mississinewa was playing at Wabash in the early sixties and Owens had the game. He called a charging foul on a Mississinewa player and as he came down the floor, the Mississinewa coach yelled, "Ref, you stink."

Owens blew his whistle, turned to the coach and signaled a technical foul. The Wabash player hit the free one, took the ball out of bounds and scored.

But as Owens went by the bench on his way down the floor, the Mississinewa coach grinned and yelled, "Hey, ref, you're smelling better all the time."

Coach Bob Warner was a favorite of all referees in eastern Indiana and when they could pull something on him, it made their day.

In the early sixties Williamsburg was at Centerville and Owens had the game with Wayne Hinchman. Centerville Coach Jim Howell had a good team and upset the favored Yellow Jackets. Warner came into the dressing room after the game and jumped all over Hinchman, blaming him for the loss. Owens calmed him down and then decided to stick one in Warner's ribs.

The referee had the Williamsburg game at home the next night so he took the two contracts he had for games with Warner later in the season and put them in his suitcase. When he arrived at the gym he told Principal Charlie Dickerson what he had planned. Dickerson thought it was a great idea.

Warner walked into the dressing room and greeted Owens.

But instead of the warm reception he expected, Warner saw Owens had a frown on his face.

"Gee, Junior," said the coach, "I'm sorry if you are upset about my getting on Wayne last night."

"Bob," said the referee, "I don't have to work for coaches who tear up referees for no reason. I can work for gentlemen." With that, he handed the coach the two contracts and said, "After tonight, I won't be back."

Warner was flustered. He tried to apologize, but Owens turned his back, knowing he could not hide his smile. The principal popped in with, "Bob, I told you this was going to happen. Your mouth gets you in trouble and you know it."

"Look," said Warner, "I promise I will not move from that bench and let blood run down my chin before I criticize you once."

"Well," said the referee, "I'll give you one more chance. Okay, I'll work the contract games, but you keep your promise."

Did he do so? "No," laughed Owens, "within minutes after the game started, Warner was on his feet, shouting at the referees, ripping his felt hat off his head and slamming it to the floor and in general, being the guy we all loved to work for."

Kids say the darnedest things. Referees are not excluded from these remarks. Carl Fleetwood, who carried a little excess weight around the middle, was working with Owens in a mid-sixties game at Hartford City when he called a foul and went running toward the bench to signal the call.

A young boy in the front row next to the bench, yelled, "You tell 'em sausage, you got the guts."

Fleetwood turned to the boy, rubbed his head and said, "You're all right, kid," and resumed the game.

Fleetwood also was quick on the comeback when he was ask to interpret a call in a game at Bluffton.

Charlie Northam was the lead official and it was a hotly contested game. A loose ball at the center circle caused a pile up of players, and Fleetwood blew his whistle for a jump ball. But the crowd was roaring so loud, Northam did not hear it and when the ball popped out of the pile, a Bluffton player grabbed it, drove under for a lay up, hit it and was fouled.

Fleetwood hurried over to Northam and said, "Charlie, I got a jump ball at the center circle."

"No you don't," answered the senior referee. "I've got a field goal and a blocking foul, and it sticks."

After the game, an elderly man came up to Fleetwood and said, "Sir, I would like to ask you a question. Didn't you signal a jump ball at center before that basket was made and a foul called?"

"Yes, sir, I did," answered the referee. "But the rule book says that the more severe call prevails over the lesser. The blocking foul that Mr. Northam called was more severe than the tie-up call I whistled."

The man was satisfied with the answer and thanked Fleetwood for explaining it to him.

When he left, the referee turned to his partner, grinned, and asked, "Do you suppose I should have told him both actions have to be simultaneous?"

Making friends with the coaches often gives a rookie referee the chance to move up to bigger games, especially when the coaches, themselves, move up.

One of the state's best was Barney Scott, then at Hagerstown. Owens worked several games for him there, so when Scott moved to the much bigger school at Jasper in 1958 and on to Seymour in 1961, he moved Owens into the big time. It proved a tremendous boost for the young referee and contributed highly to his working three state finals.

Getting your first regional is an exciting and nervous time for a young referee. The jitters end the moment that ball is tossed up for the opening jump, but before that . . . butterflies.

Bob Showalter was assigned his first regional at the huge Fort Wayne Coliseum in 1962 and was working with Owens in the second afternoon game. The two referees finished dressing for the game and while Owens relaxed, Showalter paced the floor.

"Junior," said the young referee, "let's go for a walk."

"Sure," answered Owens, thinking that might be one way to calm him down.

They started walking around the outer walk way that runs inside the building. The fire exit doors do not have glass in them so they walked halfway around before coming to the main entrance with its big glass doors and windows.

"Gee," said Showalter, looking outside, "it's still daylight."

"Bobby," said the senior referee, "it is only one o'clock in the afternoon."

Owens said that it was true, the minute the game started Showalter was all right and did a fine job of refereeing.

A similar but even more embarrassing situation happened to Dave Habegger during the first afternoon game of the 1966 state finals at Hinkle Fieldhouse.

"I had the final night game that year," said Owens, "and decided to watch the afternoon games from seats reserved for the officials next to the scorer's bench. I knew Dave was nervous since this was his first state tourney so when the announcer had us stand for the National Anthem, I stepped over next to him to show my support. As the song started, Dave cupped his hand to his mouth and said, 'Homer, move around behind me and see if it shows. I just wet my pants.' Fortunately his jock strap saved the day for it did not show and he did a fine job of refereeing."

It was not unusual for two referees to work a tournament which had three games on Thursday, two on Friday and three on Saturday. Hilligoss worked with Owens in such a marathon at Anderson and when it was over, Owens discovered he had lost nine pounds in three days.

No matter how many times a referee worked a regional or a semistate, the week before the tourney was an anxious time while waiting for that letter to arrive, specifying the assignment.

In the spring of 1949, McBride received his letter and called Hilligoss to see where he was going. No one answered the phone. So, McBride crawled in his car and drove to Hilligoss' home. There in the mailbox was the much coveted letter, so McBride stuck it in his coat pocket and went home.

Later in the day his phone rang. It was Hilligoss.

"Did you hear from the IHSAA on your semifinal assignment?" he asked.

"Sure did," answered McBride, "I'm going to Bloomington."

"Darn," said Hilligoss, "I haven't gotten mine. Do you suppose it could have been lost in that train wreck over at Dunreith yesterday?"

"Might be," answered his partner, "or maybe they decided to get younger men this year."

"Hey," he yelled into the phone, "there is no way I won't get an assignment." Then more quietly, "Is there?"

"All I know is, I got mine and you did not."

"Look," said Hilligoss, desperation in his voice, "would you ride over to Dunreith with me and see if there was a mail car on that train?"

"Sure, but I'll drive. I'll be right there to pick you up."

When Hilligoss answered the doorbell, McBride said, "Well, what do you know, the mailman delivered your letter to my address. Here it is."

"No way," yelled Hilligoss. "McBride, no way."

He quickly opened his letter and when McBride asked him where he was going, Hilligoss answered, "I'll tell you this. I'm not going with you and I'm glad."

Fans can be fickle. The quiet teller of the local bank, or the little old lady who sits serenely on her porch knitting, or the local service station operator with the big smile, can become tyrants once a basketball game starts.

Scoop Campbell, Frank Sanders and Art Gross had the Huntington sectional in the mid-fifties. The host team played in the first game and it had no more than started when this bellowing voice was heard above the entire crowd.

"Hey Scoop," it echoed throughout the gym, "get in the game. It's called basketball you know. Art, you're not any better. Learn the rules. Oh, what a lousy call. Where are you guys from?" And on and on and on.

"We talked about it at halftime," said Campbell, "and when we went back to the floor, asked the Huntington coach about the guy. We were told he was at every home game and knew every referee by his first name and the yelling never stopped."

After the second game had ended, the referees changed clothes and walked out their dressing room door. A man was standing there and they realized it was the fan with the loud voice.

"He told us he wanted to meet us personally," said Campbell, "and that we did an excellent job of refereeing. We hardly could believe it, but he was an extremely nice man away from the floor. But during a game, he was a butcher."

McBride was a master at the quick comeback with fans, often ending a problem before it began.

Three men were on the Richmond official through the first period at Alexandria and as the quarter ended, the referee stood some ten feet from them.

"Hey, McBride," one of them yelled, "did you pay to get in here?"

The referee walked closer to them and answered, "No, did you?"

"Yeh, sure did," they said in unison.

"Then" said the referee, "I am going to take home some of your admission money so you say anything you want to say." They did not yell at the referee the rest of the evening.

Coach Howard Sharpe, the winningest coach in Indiana history, said there were times when he tried and tried to get a technical to fire up his team, but the referees would not give him one.

"But the fastest I ever saw a technical called," said the Terre Haute coach, "was at home against Brazil. Babe Wheeler was the Brazil coach and the game always was a hard-fought contest between two bitter rivals.

"Wheeler was up and down all night," he recalled, "but the referees simply would not pay any attention to him. Late in the third quarter, out of sheer frustration, Wheeler hit one of the referees in the back with a crushed plastic cup and before that cup hit the floor, Wheeler had his T.

"But it didn't do him any good," Sharpe grinned. "We still won."

Sharpe had this to say about referees. "Several were good, a few outstanding and some had no business being on the floor. McBride knew the rules, believed in himself and was in complete charge of the game. You had to play basketball, for he would take nothing off of you.

"Charlie Fouty was cocky, but he did not make bad decisions. When he spoke, you listened. He thought he was the best and he controlled a game.

"C.N. Phillips was in a class by himself. He was great with kids and they loved to play for him. Very consistent.

"Dee Williams may well have been the best. He could not only handle the action on the floor, but he had the respect of the kids and the coaches.

"There are many others I could name, Marvin Todd, Dick Jacobs and Cy Birge, for example, but it is impossible to name them all."

Many referees considered the old Hartford City gymnasium the pits for working a ballgame.

"The crowd was right on top of you," said McBride, "and they made it very uncomfortable, many times when their own team was winning."

"I had the most unusual incident of my career happen in Hartford City," said referee Glen Wisler. "Midway through the third quarter a woman had a heart attack in the stands and died. The game was stopped until medics arrived, but I knew we had to finish playing or we, the refs, would have been lynched.

"Also," he recalled, "there was a swimming pool near our dressing room and after a game we often locked the door and went skinny dipping for a few minutes before showering and getting dressed."

If a coach and referee happen to be close friends, how do you handle it in a tournament if one is assigned to work the other's game?

"Carefully," laughed Wisler. "It was an early sixties regional at Fort Wayne and my close friend Bob Macy had his Albion team in the tourney and I had his game. I walked out with my partner, Roger Emmert, who at that time was sheriff of Gibson County, and we went to the Albion bench.

"Coach," I said to Macy, "I am the senior official, Glen

Wisler from Rushville, and this is Roger Emmert from Gibson County. And your name is . . . ?"

"Macy," he said, "Bob Macy. I'm glad to meet you.

"Let's have a good game coach," Wisler said, turning away. "And it was a good game, with few fouls and no major disputes.

"But to this day," he laughed, "my sheriff partner, nor the fans, nor the opposing coach, ever knew Bob and I were close friends."

There were coaches who got completely carried away in the heat of a game, or even in the dressing room at halftime. They seldom realized how humorous some of these incidents were to the officials.

Dick Jacobs was working with Norm Shields at Quincy in Owen County and the officials room was next to the host school's dressing room. The walls were little more than paper.

"Quincy's starting five included identical twins," said Jacobs, "and you certainly could not tell them apart, except for their numbers. Norm and I had settled into our chairs at halftime to rest and drink a Coke when we heard Coach Paul Hurst come into the room next to us.

"Hurst was excited and his voice high pitched as he said, 'Which twin are you, Jim or John?' 'I'm John.'

" 'Well, it's Jim I want to talk to. No, that's the wrong number. It is John.'

" 'At least I think it is John. Oh hell, you're both lazy as sin.'

" 'And as for you, you big redheaded oaf,' yelling at his center, 'you missed two put backs . . . you missed two put backs . . . you missed two put backs.' "

" 'But coach,' the referees heard, breaking up with laughter, 'that's six . . . I didn't miss that many!' "

Referees who worked with McBride said the unusual seemed to follow him around and they were ready for anything at anytime.

The 1961 Bluffton sectional draw found the two favorites in the first afternoon game on Saturday. Bill May and Bob Henne had the game and McBride was to work the second outing.

McBride came walking into the dressing room as Henne and May were lacing up their shoes, ready to go to the floor.

"This Ossian-Bluffton game should be a good one," he told the two referees. "I think I will get dressed and sit by the scorers bench to watch it."

The two referees went to the floor and did not give McBride a second thought.

At Bluffton, the announcer had a booming voice, and introducing the Tigers was a major production. The lights in the gymnasium would be shut off and a spotlight aimed at the entry door. On a given signal, the announcer would bellow, "And now . . . introducing the mighty Bluffton Tigers . . . at forward . . . " and the spotlight flooded the doorway.

There, walking through the door, in the glare of the spotlight and the roar of the crowd, came . . . Don McBride!

The game between Rushville and Lawrenceburg had been hot and heavy. By the time it was over, Referees John Gwin and McBride were worn out.

As they sat in the dressing room to rest, before taking showers, the telephone rang. McBride answered it.

"Who won?" an anxious voice asked.

McBride answered, "If you had been here you would know," and hung up.

John Collier, head coach at Brookville, had a bad habit of keeping his players in the huddle long after the horn sounded to start action. McBride warned Collier again and again, but it did little good.

Finally, McBride decided to teach him a lesson. After the second horn had sounded and the Brookville team did not come onto the floor, the referee laid the ball on the floor and told the opposing team captain, "Pick it up when you are ready to go."

"You mean we can throw it in before they get out here?"

"Right . . . time starts right now."

The boy reached down, grabbed the ball, tossed it to a forward near the basket and he scored uncontested. Collier saw what happened and came rushing at McBride. "Hey, Mac, you can't do that. We were not on the floor."

"John," answered the referee, "I warned you time and again about breaking up your huddle when the second horn sounded. Now, maybe, you have learned your lesson. Let's play." Collier did not like it, but from that time on, when the second horn sounded his players hurried to their positions.

McBride did get himself in trouble by trying to be funny. Pendleton had an excellent team and Fortville little or nothing when the two met. So, the Fortville coach decided to have his players hold the ball and the Pendleton coach told his players to let them do so.

For the first quarter there was no action. During the break a janitor brought a folding chair out to the center line for McBride, and he made the mistake of sitting down during the second period.

The Fortville coach did not think it was funny and reported the referee to the IHSAA.

The next evening the telephone rang at McBride's home.

It was Commissioner Phillips. "Don, I understand you are pretty good as a referee, but I heard you refereed a game while seated in a chair."

McBride tried to explain but was cut off by Phillips who said, "Don't do it again," and hung up.

At halftime of a fast-paced game it was not unusual for one or both of the referees to nod off in the dressing room as they rested.

McBride was officiating with Jim Ridge and two of the top rivals of Randolph County, Spartanburg and Lynn, had gone full speed the first half. The dressing room was the teachers lounge and there were cots along two walls, so the referees stretched out. They were calmly snoring away when Lynn Principal Will (Chick) Moore came hurrying in yelling, "Hey you two. We are past time to start. Come on, wake up."

The two referees tossed cold water on their faces and hurried to the gym. McBride said, "That never happened again."

Discretion on the part of a referee often paid off, causing a fan to change his or her mind about the official.

The game was at Liberty and each time McBride would make a call against the host team a man under the basket would yell, "Wrong call McBride."

As the game progressed the fan was becoming more and more obnoxious, adding a few expletives to his "wrong call" philosophy. With two minutes to go until halftime, Liberty called a time-out and an Indiana state trooper seated a short distance from the obnoxious fan, had had enough. He came over to the man, took his arm and said, "Let's go. You are out of here."

McBride was standing nearby and knew the trooper. He quickly walked over and said, "No, don't make him leave. He may be right part of the time."

"If you say so," answered the trooper. "There is no reason for him to be on your back all the time."

"Thanks anyhow," the referee answered, returning to his position.

The fan never uttered another word. Had he been ejected, McBride would have had an enemy for life.

When a referee backs out of working a game at the last minute, or becomes ill, it puts lots of undue pressure on the other official.

McBride had just closed his suitcase and started putting on his jacket when the telephone at his home rang. It was the referee who was to work the Boston-College Corner game at Boston. He informed McBride he could not make it and hung up.

So the Richmond referee hurried the eight miles to the Wayne County school and told Principal Harry Winters he would have to work the game alone as the second referee had backed out at the last minute. Winters was not happy, but he agreed.

Of all nights the game went to double overtime, and by the time McBride reached the dressing room, he was totally bushed. As he was sitting on a chair, catching his breath before taking a shower, in walked the principal.

"Don," he said, "you did a tremendous job tonight, and I want to give you extra pay for your work."

McBride had to smile to himself as the principal handed him a one dollar bill.

Only once did McBride arrive at a game to discover part of his uniform was missing. His young daughter had the bad habit of opening his suitcase and taking things out without his realizing what was happening.

He had reached the Middletown gymnasium, headed to the dressing room and started to get ready, when he realized his shirt was missing. It was too far to go back for it, and the Middletown principal said he couldn't help, so McBride decided to borrow one of the shirts worn by the B-team referees in the first game.

The problem was, both B-team referees were much smaller than the Richmond official and neither shirt came close to fitting.

"That may well have been the only game in history," said McBride, "where the senior official wore a bare midriff."

There are times when a call must be reversed. And it takes a good referee to admit he is wrong, no matter the wrath he might get from the fans.

Referee Bill May's father, Wilbur, also was an official for many years. He was working with McBride in a 1946 game at Liberty in Union County and there was a rule that said, if a ball bounced off the floor and into the goal it was not counted.

A Liberty player took a long shot and Wilbur called a foul on the College Corner guard. He quickly turned to see if the shot went in and sure enough, it was dropping through the nets. So, May signalled two points. He was directly in front of the College Corner bench and immediately the coach protested the call, saying the ball bounced off the floor.

May, excellent referee that he was, walked over to McBride and asked, "Did it hit the floor, Mac?" "Yes it did."

May headed to the scorers bench and ruled the shot no good. The Liberty crowd roared their disapproval but the referee knew he was right in reversing his call.

There were some referees who simply could not work together. McBride found this true with a man named John Magnabosco who believed in the old adage, "No blood, no call." The official was a football coach at Ball State University in Muncie and the rougher the basketball game, the happier he became.

The two referees were working at Winchester and the game had become a knock down, drag out affair. By halftime, McBride had had enough and confronted the football coach.

"Maggie," asked McBride, "don't you think you ought to call a foul once in awhile?"

"No way, McBride," he answered. "They are having fun so let them play."

"But what about the rules," McBride countered.

"Rules are made to be broken," said the football coach, and McBride never worked another game with him after that night.

Later the Richmond referee said, "If the rules of the IHSAA were not to be followed, then they would not have been written in the first place. I am a firm believer the rules of the game must rule over everything else. This does not mean there cannot be interpretations of those rules that may vary, but a rule is a rule."

It was very unusual for a referee to have a game at the town where he lived, or the school from which he had been graduated. But it happened to Gene McNutt and ended in a big surprise for both him and McBride.

McNutt's father had a grocery store in Williamsburg and after each home game, referees, coaches, fans or whoever, would gather there to eat sandwiches, drink Cokes and talk basketball.

Williamsburg was host to Milton and it turned out to be not only a close game won by the visitors, but a game where neither McBride nor McNutt did a good job. The two schools were undefeated so tensions ran high. Fans at both ends booed most every call and when there was a no call on the final shot by a Williamsburg player that clinched it for Milton, the fans really let the two referees have it.

As they were dressing after the game, McNutt said, "I hate to go down to the store but that last call was not a foul, so how about it?"

"Sure," answered McBride, "they can't any more than scalp us."

The two referees got in McNutt's car and drove to the grocery. As they approached the front door they saw the store was packed solid with people. They parked and walked to the front door."

"Well," said McNutt, "here goes nothing."

He turned the handle on the door but it didn't move. He tried it again and still it would not open.

"Well I'll be damned," McNutt said, "Dad has locked us out."

And those inside did not open the door, so the two referees tucked their tails and headed home.

Referees have said for years that coaches are like elephants, they never forget.

Tim Heller was the assistant coach at Sunman and in a county tourney game he kept screaming at Homer Owens that the opposing team's center was moving his foot every time he pivoted to shoot. The referee warned him to quiet down and informed him the center was holding his position and there was no reason to call a traveling violation.

Virtually every time Owens passed the bench, Heller would say, "He's still doing it."

But the referee decided to ignore the coach and the game ended without a technical.

A year later, Union in Randolph County needed a coach and Owens was on the advisory board. He suggested Heller to the members and they told him to give the coach a call and see if he was available.

Heller answered the phone and Owens told him he was sure the Union job would be his if he was interested. They talked for several minutes and it was decided Heller would come to Union the next day for an interview.

As he started to hang up, Heller thanked the referee for the job offer and then added, "By the way, Homer, that kid still traveled."

New Rules Under Consideration

New rules for high school basketball play are being considered on an annual basis. Here are nine changes under discussion for future implementation.

1. Eliminating the alternate possession rule on tie-ups and blocked shots. Several alternatives being studied, including return of the jump ball.

2. Changing penalty for an intentional foul to make it stronger.

3. Using a thirty or forty-five second clock to restrict team control in the forecourt. In other words, a shot clock.

4. Allowing a sixth personal foul for eligible players when the game goes into overtime.

5. Stopping the clock after any successful field goal in the last minute of play.

6. Prohibiting substitutions following a successful free throw.

7. Mandating that players wear a tooth and mouth protector.

8. Restricting to five the number of players along a free throw lane during a foul shot attempt.

9. Requiring players to take position along the lane for first free throw if they want that position for a second attempt.

Perhaps none of these rules ever will be adopted while others, now in use, may be changed to make the game better.

The National Federation Basketball Rules Committee sends out five hundred questionnaires to coaches and five hundred to officials prior to its annual meeting each year. The results are presented at this meeting and considered when rule changes are discussed.

The last time a year passed without at least one new rule being added was 1933.

5

Phillips & Phillips, No Relation

C.N. Phillips ranks in the top five when the history of Indiana basketball officiating is discussed by Golden Age referees and coaches. He started refereeing in 1929 and Omer (Ham) Werneke helped him get his start. He refereed for twenty years.

L.V. Phillips was in his first year as commissioner of the IHSAA when C.N. Phillips was assigned his first state finals. The year was 1945.

"I took a lot of ribbing from officials and friends alike over that one," laughed Phillips. "I was not related to the commissioner, but the fact our last names were Phillips and we both used initials instead of names, opened the door for the needle to be used."

He and T.R. Smith worked all three games in the 1945 finals, held in the coliseum at the Indiana State Fairgrounds.

C.N. was back in 1946 and had an afternoon game as well as the final ballgame. He considered it an honor to have been the referee in that championship game when one of the greats of Indiana history, "Jumpin" Johnny Wilson, led his Anderson Indians to victory.

On his return to the final game in 1949, Phillips said the mediocre record of Jasper indicated the final game might be a walkaway for Madison. But Jasper Coach Cabby O'Neal had other ideas. Jasper went head to head with Madison from the opening whistle and Phillips said he and his partner, Roland Baker, had their hands full.

"Jasper had a boy named White," said Phillips, "and he was the shortest player on the floor. Cabby told White to drive for the basket as often as possible and the youngster responded with twenty points, a good number in those days.

"But," said Phillips, "if White was covered, Cabby had a sparkplug kid at the other guard named Schutz who fired in five long ones that kept Madison loose. It proved more than Coach Ray Eddy and his Madison players could handle and Jasper walked away with the title, 62-61.

"I realized I would not get another state finals," said Phillips, "so I decided to hang it up. I had had a good twenty years, done all I wanted to do, and it was time to quit and become a spectator."

He did just that. In fact, Phillips holds a record that may someday be broken, but it is doubtful. He attended sixty-two consecutive Indiana Basketball State Tournament finals from 1930 to 1992. Those who were close to him knew he considered this the highest achievement of his life.

Phillips had a relative by marriage, Maurice (Mo) Kennedy, who was considered one of the top coaches of the state. He often chided Phillips for not working some of his games.

"Mo," said the referee, "just be thankful I won't work your games. If I did, you would not have as good a record as you now have."

If a fan continues to be obnoxious, especially if he has had a couple belts prior to the game, it often takes logic to find a satisfactory conclusion. McBride tells this story:

"Wayne Hinchman was coaching at Winchester in Randolph County in the forties and Hilligoss and I worked the game with Union City. One of Winchester's biggest followers, and loudest booster, was Walter Wine, a member of the sectional championship team Kennedy had coached there several years earlier. The longer the game went, the louder Wine became. And, after having time to slip outside at halftime for a few more nips, Wine was in rare form as the third period started.

"I kept glancing into the crowd," said McBride, "and I know everyone wondered what I was going to do. There was no way we could allow the screaming to continue, for it was ruining the game. There was a tie up at one end of the floor and the Union City coach called a time-out."

McBride walked to the edge of the wall that surrounded the gym, got up on a bench and yelled at Wine.

"Walter, stand up." Wine stood up. "Tell me how come you know more about this game than we do."

"Why I played on Mo Kennedy's team in '27 and we had a great team," Wine yelled back.

"Did you win the holiday tourney?" asked McBride.

"Sure did," Wine answered.

"How about the sectional?" McBride called.

"Won that too," yelled back Wine.

"Then what did your team do?" asked the referee. "We played Muncie in the regional," Wine hollered.

McBride paused for several seconds, and you could have heard a pin drop, then he asked, "Who won?"

"Why . . . " Wine started to answer, stopped in mid-sentence, looked around at the crowd . . . and sat down.

"End of problem," laughed McBride.

How important is the attentive action of a referee in determining the final outcome of a game? Ask any coach and he can come up with a moment in an important game where the decision or indecision of a referee made a huge difference.

Coach Howard Sharpe always will remember the 1953 state finals when the names of twins Harley and Arley Andrews and Uncle Harold were known in every corner of Indiana.

"We defeated Richmond in the afternoon," said Sharpe, "and entered the championship game with a record of 31-2. Only South Bend Central stood between Terre Haute Gerstmeyer and the title I believed we richly deserved. In fact, I felt we had beaten twelve teams that year that were better than Central.

"But in the final game, Central played like all-stars and with seventeen seconds left in the fourth quarter, we trailed, 42-41. In those days, the clock continued to run when the ball was out of bounds, and at that seventeen-second mark, we managed to flip the ball away from a Central player on a dribble and it rolled directly to the referee out of bounds.

"The referee, Dominic Polizotto," said Sharpe, "grabbed the ball and instead of giving it to my player at that spot, rolled it across the floor to the other referee on the opposite side. To this day, I do not know why this was done, but since it was a referee decision, I could do nothing about it. As the ball was thrown in, the clock now showed four seconds to play. Harley took a hurried shot in that final four seconds but it hit the front of the rim and bounced away.

"I do not know whether we would have won or not," said the retired coach, "but if we had been given the full seventeen seconds that we should have had, we certainly would have had a better chance."

The next year the IHSAA Rules Committee changed the rule, stopping the clock on such a play.

Referee Bob Spay was working the regional at Terre Haute, and he walked over to the bench to get the captain from Coach Sharpe. Before he could ask, the coach said, "You want to know how this game will come out?"

"You got the scoop?" Spay asked. "It hasn't even started yet."

"Don't make no difference," said Sharpe, "we beat them early in the season but since then, they have improved and we have not. So, they will win this one by six or seven points."

"Well Sharpie," said the official, "if you know that for a fact, why don't you just call this game off 'cause I got another one to work tonight and I could use the rest."

"No sir," said the Terre Haute coach, "I don't care how

bad they beat us, we are happy to be in the regional and we are going to play this game."

"You know what?" Spay said. "Terre Haute lost by seven points."

It is vital for referees to stay up with rule changes. But some picked them up as the new season got underway, much to the despair of the more meticulous veterans. Dick Jacobs tells this story:

"I picked up referee Roland Baker to work our first game of the season. We had not gone a mile when Roland asked, 'what changes are there in the rules?' I glanced at him in disbelief and said, you mean you haven't read them? 'No,' said Baker, 'I hate reading those things. Just tell me what they are and I'll work them out as we go.' "

Referees who were tops in handling touchy situations, usually did so in a quiet, yet firm manner.

Danny Jacobs was working with Gabby Byers in 1956 at Scottsburg and the coach was giving Byers fits. Every time the referee got near the bench, it was a replay of the last time down the floor, gripe, gripe, gripe.

At a time-out, the two referees got together and Jacobs asked, "What in the world is wrong with him?"

"I don't know," answered Byers, "but I am going to fix him the next time he gets on me. If I stop play, come over and listen to a lesson in taking charge."

The second quarter started without incident as the host team came down the floor. But a shot missed and on the rebound, Byers called a foul on Scottsburg. Off the bench came the coach, roaring in protest and slamming a sweat jacket to the floor. Byers slowly walked to the bench and Jacobs followed.

"Mr. Coach," drawled Byers, "I got something I want to tell you and you listen. The good guys tonight are wearing white [the opposing team] and they are going to shoot two free throws and get the ball out of bounds. Do you understand this signal?" And he flattened his right palm over his left extended fingers, a technical.

Butler Fieldhouse The Best

Butler Fieldhouse, now known as Hinkle Fieldhouse, was home to the Indiana High School Basketball championship series from 1928 to 1971, except for the war years of 1943-44-45 when the final three games were played at the Indiana State Fair Coliseum. When asked what gymnasium ranks No. 1 in the state, a great majority of Golden Age referees listed Hinkle. Here are their reasons:

"You were isolated from the fans, due to size of the fieldhouse, and even the coaches and players were off the floor and out of the way."

"There was excellent room to work the sidelines and ends without worrying about running into someone."

"The floor was solid and had no dead spots. This was surprising since it was a removeable floor."

"The lighting was excellent with none of the dark areas that often were found in other gymnasiums."

"When you went to the bench, you got the right answer. Men such as timer Jim Morris knew the rules and you never had to question a decision."

"When you walked onto the floor you immediately were involved in a frenzied atmosphere. You did not have to see it, you felt it."

"All referees will remember Charley McIlfresh in the equipment cage downstairs. He ruled over his domain with a passion, bellowing at any referee who showed up for the game ball or towels, but always with a twinkle in his eye."

Hinkle will forever be the Basketball Cathedral on 49th Street.

Jacobs said the coach looked at Byers, shrugged his shoulders and sat down. He caused no more problems.

Butler Coach Tony Hinkle, a former referee himself, often spoke at the yearly officials clinic, and one theme he always got across became a pattern for Dick Jacobs.

"Tony told us, 'If you ever referee a game at Butler, do not glad hand me. I do not want a politician for a referee. Be professional, call the game, take a shower and go home. And, during the game, leave nothing to doubt.'

"That was my philosophy as long as I refereed," said Jacobs. "There were some, like McBride and Fouty, who were exactly opposite, and that was their style. Mine was to call the best game possible and then go home."

Dick and Danny Jacobs took part in a 1971 medical study by Dr. John Hollan of Indiana University, to determine different functions of a referee's heart during a basketball game. It was sanctioned by the IHSAA office and resulted in some unusual findings.

"Dr. Hollan attached wires to our bodies," said Danny, "and a man on the sideline monitored our heart during the ball game."

"My biggest surprise," said Dick, "came when they played the Star-Spangled Banner before the game got underway and our heart rates made a sudden climb."

"Some coaches were concerned that wearing the wires would interfere with our job of refereeing," said Danny, "but we assured them it would not, and it didn't."

When the six referees who took part in the study saw the results published in 1972, they were surprised at the constant changing of their heart rhythm, elevation of their pulse and the evolving stress level as the game progressed, especially if it was a hard fought contest or one where both teams often used the fast break.

Dick Jacobs often worked with his younger brother Danny and both had final tournament assignments, Dick working two and his brother one. Dick was Mr. Steady while

Danny was the talker, belonging more to the McBride, Fouty mode.

"Our working together gave us a chance to talk over the game on the way home, or laugh at the odd things that happened," said Danny. He continued:

"One night at Booneville, we tossed the son of the superintendent out of the game and it gave the coach a chance to find out how good two other players were.

"This kid, because of being the superintendent's son or just built that way, gave us trouble from the first play. I warned him a couple times to watch his mouth, but he kept right on disputing every call we made.

"So, just before the first quarter ended, I'd had enough and I tossed him out. The crowd really got on me, but I noticed the coach did not say very much.

"At halftime no one would speak to us. A student manager brought us Cokes, where normally it is the principal or another school official, and we drank them in silence. Not one visitor showed up.

"The final two quarters went fine, Booneville won and we were in the dressing room finishing up when in walked the coach with a grin on his face.

"Fellows," he said, "thank you. I finally got a chance to find out who else can play that position."

A similar incident happened at Kokomo when Danny booted one of the Kats' better players, one who constantly griped at every call and was obnoxious on the floor. At the end of the third quarter, Kokomo Coach Joe Platt told Danny, 'I want to see you after the game.'

"Well, I knew I was going to get my butt chewed," said Danny, "for Joe was well known to do that on occasion. But much to my surprise, he walked into the dressing room after the game, shook my hand and said, 'I am glad you took care of my player, 'cause I have decided I won't have to take care of him the rest of the year.'

"I did not work another game with Kokomo that year," said Danny, "but I guessed that one obnoxious young man saw the rest of the season from afar. When Joe Platt made up his mind, no one changed it."

Do referees hear the fans when they are working games? "Most certainly," said Danny. "I was working the afternoon game of the state finals and spotted IU Coach Bob Knight sitting with Huntington Coach Bob Straight. A few nights later, I went to IU to work a scrimmage game for Knight and the coach greeted me with, "I hollered at you the other day at the state finals."

"Yeh, coach," drawled Danny, "you and 17,000 others." Jacobs added, "Knight got a good laugh out of that."

As mentioned earlier, Johnnie Baratto was king at firing up his team with a technical. The referees knew this and tried their best not to put one on him, but, in most cases, the coach would make sure he acted up badly enough to get the tech.

"I had East Chicago Washington and Kokomo in the afternoon game of the 1962 state finals," said Dick Jacobs, "and was working with Scoop Campbell. We both knew Baratto's tactics and we both knew there would be a breaking point if he started.

"We got through the first half without major problems, but Joe Platt had his Kats playing smooth basketball and seemed to be in control. We remarked during the break, how calm Baratto had been but Scoopy said, 'It may be the calm before the storm.'

"He was right," Jacobs continued. "Early in the third quarter, Kokomo went on a roll and the next thing we knew, the Kats were up by fourteen points. During the run, after he had loudly questioned a foul call, I had told Baratto to sit down on the bench and calm himself.

"Then it happened. I called a charge on a Washington player and there was no doubt the boy did charge as the Kokomo player was in position and standing flatfooted. Off the bench came Baratto in a rage, screaming at me in words that degraded my ancestors and I put a T on him.

"It was all he needed," continued the referee. "One

of his players named Miles, started hitting long shots like he owned Butler Fieldhouse and, although Kokomo fought with everything they had, with a minute to go, East Chicago went in front by one point. As the game ended, the ball was being batted around on the Kokomo bankboard but Baratto had won.

"We were in the shower room after the game," said Jacobs, "when East Chicago's assistant coach came walking in. The showers at Butler have a rim around the outside and often water builds up around your feet. The assistant stepped into the shower, water going over his shoes, and said, 'Coach Baratto wanted me to shake your hands and tell you that both of you called a tremendous game . . . and he especially wanted to thank you, Mr. Jacobs, for that technical foul.' "

Dick said he turned to Scoopy and said with a grin, "That SOB did it to me again."

Joe Mullins also had his go at Baratto, and at least one time, came out ahead.

"The game was at East Chicago," said Mullins, "and I knew Baratto was a character, so I was waiting for him. Early in the third period, one of his players traveled. When I motioned for the ball, he turned and tossed it the other way. I immediately whistled a technical.

"As I headed to the scorer's bench to make sure the T was recorded, I heard Baratto screaming over my shoulder. When I finished at the table, I turned toward the coach. He shouted, 'What happened? What happened?' I told him I asked for the ball and his player threw it the other way," continued Mullins. 'Never saw that call in my life,' yelled Baratto. 'Never saw that call in my life.'

"Well, coach," said Mullins, walking away, "you have now!"

Glen Wisler had his run-in with Baratto and came away realizing the coach wanted no disruptions in play.

The game was at Michigan City and the host coach, Doug Adams, questioned an over-the-line call by Wisler's partner, Stan Dubis. Wisler called an official time out and was explaining the call to Adams when Baratto came rushing up.

"What's going on?" he demanded.

"I am explaining the over-the-line rule to Coach Adams," said Wisler.

"Ref," yelled Baratto, "we don't need a rules clinic around here. Let's play basketball."

"Dubis, by the way," said Wisler, "has the distinction of being the only referee ever to be hit in the head with a cigarette lighter thrown from the crowd. It knocked him cold and he had to have stitches before resuming the game. But he did finish."

Getting firm with a coach often avoided a technical. Wisler was good at doing this. "Muncie Central was playing Logansport, and as usual, Central Coach Ike Tallman was up screaming from the opening tip, while Logan Coach Jim Jones was his usual composed self. Four times, on fast breaks, Muncie players would pass off and then run right over the opposing players.

"I called charging each time and each time Tallman let me have it full force. Finally, I had enough. But instead of giving him a T, I went over, quieted him down and told him he knew better than that. I said to tell his boys to cut it out. He did and that was the end of the problem. Had I given him a technical, it would have been nothing but chaos the rest of the game."

Wisler considers Coach Les Ray, then at New Castle, one of the true gentlemen of the game. "New Castle was at Elwood and during a time-out, the Elwood coach came to me and said that when his players stepped out of bounds to throw in the ball under the New Castle basket, boys sitting there were jerking the hairs out of the players' legs.

"I went down to talk to the boys and here came Les, wanting to know what was wrong. I told him. He turned to the line of boys, his B-team players, and said, 'If you are doing it, stop it right now. If I see any of you reaching for an Elwood player, you will spend the rest of the night on the bus.' It stopped immediately," said Wisler.

Wisler and Bill Hile had an odd thing happen at Fort Wayne Central. "Attucks was Central's opponent," said Wisler, "and several times during the first half, Herb Banet, Central coach, loudly questioned calls, but made it through the half without a T. But in the third quarter, Bill called a charging foul on a Central player and Banet leaned back on the bench in despair. As he threw his arms up in disgust, he let go of the note cards he was holding. They scattered all over the place and I ran toward him to signal a technical. But before I could get there, the coach jumped to his feet and ran out the side exit. No coach, no technical," said Wisler.

"After the game, Banet came into the dressing room and said, 'Fellas, you couldn't put one on me if I wasn't there to accept it, could you?' He laughed all the way out the door."

If a referee is a veteran, and the coach is in his first few years of varsity action, it is not unusual for the veteran official to give the younger man advice. Sometimes it is followed, sometimes it is not.

Pat Malaska was coach at Fairmount in Grant County, and Joe Mullins had John Lowell (Buz) Mertz as his partner. Buz was a veteran referee who was not the least bit timid in telling a coach off, or even getting physical when the situation called for it.

"Malaska was on both of us soon after the game started," said Mullins, "and I honestly believe there were times when he did not even realize what he was saying. I don't remember one call the entire night he agreed with.

"We were getting dressed, after the game, when the coach walked into our room," continued the referee. "He was no more than two steps inside the door when Buz grabbed him by both shoulders, gave him a shake, looked him square in the eyes and said in an intimidating voice, 'Damn you Pat . . . when you start coaching instead of officiating, you'll go a long way in this profession.' " In later years, Malaska, who became one of the state's leading coaches, said it was the best advice he ever received.

Mertz, who had been Mullins' sixth grade teacher, was instrumental in helping the young referee get his start. But he was reluctant to do so. "He tried to talk me out of it," said Mullins, "saying it took a lot of time away from home, the pay was terrible and the fans could be murder."

But Mullins persisted, although in his first game, he wondered if he had made a mistake. "Buz took me along to work the Sweetser at Swayzee game in Grant county, always a 'barn burner,' and this one was no different. In the third quarter, I had called a travel on a Swayzee player and was holding the ball out of bounds for the toss in when a Coke bottle missed my head by about three feet.

"Buz stopped the game and had the announcer page the principal. When he arrived at the bench, Buz was ready to tell him this game was over with a forfeit to Sweetser when the principal explained the situation. It turned out the person who threw the bottle was a mentally disturbed girl and he assured the referees it never would happen again.

"Even though an acceptable explanation was given," said Mullins, "I wondered for days whether I was getting into something I would regret. Instead, I found something I dearly loved."

Coaches and referees in most cases are friends off the floor. The heat of the game can change this, and often words are exchanged that would have gone better not said.

"Wayne Crispen went with me to referee a game at Warsaw, with Winamac the opponent," said Joe Mullins. "Dee Baker, the Winamac coach, was a friend and a graduate of Butler University. He came into the dressing room prior to the start, and I told him I would be working the Butler at Valparaiso college game the following Tuesday night. I said if he would like to go I would be glad to pick him up on the way. He readily agreed.

"It was a rough ball game," continued Mullins, "and in the third quarter, Wayne put a technical on a Winamac player and I found myself right in front of Baker. 'What's going on?' he yelled. 'A technical,' he screamed. 'A technical!' Then he turned to me and said, 'Joe, I'm not going with you Tuesday night. I'm not ever going with you again.'"

After the game, Crispen and Mullins were finishing dressing when Baker came sheepishly walking into the official's room. Before he had a chance to say a word, Mullins said, "Sure sorry you can't go with me Tuesday, Dee. Should be quite a game."

Baker ducked his head, grinned, shuffled his feet like a boy caught in a cookie jar, and said, "Gee, Joe. Guess I'll go after all." The two remained friends for life.

The gymnasium where Muncie Central played, even with all of its basketball tradition, was not the favorite of many referees. Joe Mullins was one of them.

"You never knew what you were going to run into at Muncie Central," said Mullins. "The dressing room was down a corridor from one end of the Walnut Street Fieldhouse and you had to walk through a crowd to get there.

"Muncie was playing Richmond and it had been a hard-fought, yet well-played first half. As soon as the horn sounded to end the half, we headed toward the corridor. Suddenly the crowd surged in ahead of us and I saw two men in a fist fight. There was no way we could get through so we stopped in our tracks.

"By this time, we were totally surrounded by fans and they were jostling us from all sides. It really was a dangerous situation," he continued.

"Just then, the biggest, burliest policeman I have ever seen in my life, brushed past me, knocking people right and left as he went. He first grabbed the fighter on the left, popped him on the head with his billy club, dropped him to the floor, and then did the same thing with the guy on the right.

"He turned to us and said with a grin, 'Guess you can go now,' and we did."

One hazard of refereeing that few fans know ever exists, is caused by a jock strap rubbing the groin area. It can be extremely painful.

"I worked the first half of a Friday night sectional game at Logansport," said Mullins, "and the farther it went, the more sore I became. By halftime, I actually was limping, it hurt so bad.

"I put powder on it during the rest period," he continued, "but it did little good. By the time the game ended, I was in sheer misery. In fact, I had grave doubts I could work the Saturday games, it was so raw.

"I had taken a shower, moaning and groaning as the water hit the galled area, when Logansport Coach Cliff Wells came into the dressing room."

" 'What's wrong with you Joe?' " he asked. " 'I saw you limping out there and you look like you are hurting.'

"I sat down in a chair," said Mullins, "and showed him the gall area. He took one look and said, 'hey, sit still. I got something that will cure that.'

"In a couple minutes he returned with a bottle of liquid and some cotton balls. He told me to spread my legs and lean back. He also told me this would burn a little and he quickly dabbed one entire side of my groin. I went straight up. I never have had anything burn so bad in my life.

"After I scraped myself off the ceiling, he did the same thing with the other groin and this time I managed to stay in my chair, although I had tears in my eyes.

"You know what?" Mullins added. "That darn stuff worked like a charm. The next morning that irritation was totally gone and I worked the finals without any problem. Come to think of it," Mullins said. "He never did tell me what he dabbed on there. It may have been his own remedy."

One of the outstanding referees for many years was Odie

Barnett. Yet, he too, became quite nervous before a game, especially if it were tournament time.

"We had the semifinals in the old fieldhouse at Indiana University in 1949," said Mullins, "and as we sat around talking in the dressing room, I noticed Odie was nervous. However, I did not know how nervous until we started to dress. Odie put on his game trousers, took them off and inspected the seams, put them back on, took them off and inspected them again, put them back on and again took them off to check out who knows what? After the fourth try, he finished dressing. This covered a period of some twenty minutes.

"Now I do not know what it did in helping calm him down," laughed Mullins, "but it sure as heck did nothing positive for me."

Like many other high-strung officials, once the game was underway, you could not find a calmer person in the gymnasium than Odie Barnett, if everything went smoothly.

Barnett also was a worrier. Before a game, he paced the floor in the dressing room, knowing something drastic was going to happen during the contest. If something did happen, no matter how minor, Odie could make it into a major development, if allowed to have his course.

Odie was working with John Thomas in an early fifties game at Pendleton and the host team was having little trouble with its opponent, Royerton. So the Pendelton coach decided to let one of his second team players get some first-team experience and tried to bring him in.

"We could not let him in the game," said Thomas, "because his name wasn't on the roster. Also, the shirt he was wearing had a B-team number and was not the exact color as the rest of the team. Odie really got upset and told me the rules said the kid couldn't enter the game. I told him to calm down, we were not going to let this be a problem.

"So, we walked over to the Pendleton coach and I asked him if the player going out would be back in the game. He told me no, the boy from the second team would finish the game. I looked at Odie and said, no problem. I pointed at the A-team player and told him to take off his jersey and give it to the other boy. He can finish the game wearing the A-player's number."

"We did, and it worked out fine, although I am sure the IHSAA might have frowned at my solution."

On another occasion, Thomas came up with a solution that the IHSAA also would have questioned, but it worked.

"Cross Plains was playing New Marion at Versailles and it was a ragged game, punctuated by many fouls," said Thomas. "Late in the fourth quarter, I called New Marion for a foul and Coach Jake Walbring came running onto the floor. 'John,' he said, 'I am out of players. I don't have any- one to send in.'

"Jake," said the referee, "I don't care what you do to finish this game, but let's get it going. Put in the student manager for all I care. So he did . . . and the kid finished the game."

Many games found the small schools without the usual ten players dressed for the varsity squad. If there were excess fouls or injuries, running out of players could not be helped.

Fountain City was in the 1954 semifinals of the Wayne County Tourney against Milton when foul calls started piling up. Homer Owens and Jim Ridge had the game and with two minutes to play, Fountain City was down to four players.

When the game ended, Coach Cloyce Quakenbush came roaring into the dressing room and tore Ridge into shreds. He paced the floor and went on and on, yet never saying one word to Owens. After he left, Ridge said, "Why did he get on me like that? You were the one who called seventy per cent of the fouls."

"Shucks Jim," said Owens, "I guess he just knows a good referee when he sees one." Ridge threw a wet towel at him.

Elkhart Coach Max Bell loved to get on the referees,

making it as much a part of a game as tossing up the ball. Glen Wisler had a chance to put him in his place. "The game was at Michigan City and I warned Max a couple of times to ease up or he was going to get a technical. Suddenly, after a call, there was Bell some six feet out on the floor, screaming my direction. I whistled the ball dead and started walking toward him. He quickly sat down on the bench. I knelt down in front of him so I could look him straight in the eye and said, 'Max, I am going to give you an early Christmas present.' He asked me what it was and I said, 'I am going to let you stay in this game. But if you get out on this floor again, you are going outdoors in a hurry.'

"I got up from my crouch," said Wisler, "and as I headed toward the end of the gym to get the ball, there were two policemen standing there. I said to them, 'fellas, is it still snowing out there? I'm a long way from home.' They told me it was and I picked up the ball.

"What I did not realize until later was that Max thought I had told the policemen to watch him and he sat as quiet as a lamb the rest of the game. A week later," continued Wisler, "I had the Elkhart game at Fort Wayne Central and here comes Bell."

"'Hey Wisler,'" he said, "'You still as mean tonight as you were the other night at Michigan City?'

"Max, my friend," said Wisler, "just try me and see!" Bell chuckled and was the perfect gentleman all evening.

Referees have been known to stretch out calling a technical to the breaking point, but there is a time when this ends.

McBride and Jack O'Neal were to work a game at Indianapolis Washington and it would be the Richmond official's first time to see Dave Hines, the Washington coach, in action. "Don," said O'Neal, "take it easy on Hines tonight. He is a young coach and tends to be nervous and flighty during a game. Also, he was graduated with my wife from high school and is a good friend."

McBride made no comment to O'Neal, but during the first half, Hines was all over the place, shouting at McBride and in general going far past his position as a coach.

At halftime, McBride said, "Jack, you better tell Hines to calm down or friend or no friend, I am going to call a technical on him."

Only three minutes were gone in the third quarter when Hines again went too far and the Richmond official whistled him for a T. From that point, Hines was a different man on the court.

"I realized afterward," said the referee, "he was testing me to see how far he could go. He found out. Since that night, Dave and I have been good friends."

Madison Coach Bud Ritter said he learned his lesson early in dealing with the Richmond referee.

"We were in a close one with Scottsburg and I yelled one too many times at Don and he put a T on me. As he went by the bench toward the opposite end of the floor for the free throw, I yelled, 'McBride, you stink.' He didn't even look at me as he headed to the other end, but when he got to the foul line, he turned toward me and yelled, 'That costs you a second one. Can you still smell me?' "

Former Commissioner Phil Eskew said McBride's greatest asset was his ability to help young officials not only learn the trade, but in assisting them to move up, if they had the right stuff.

"He had to work with an official only one time to know whether that young man had what it takes to be tops in his field," said the commissioner.

Orval (Shorty) Burdsall, coach at Alexandria, gave McBride one of his finest compliments.

"Don," said Burdsall, "could have been ever bit as good a coach as he was a referee. He had the natural instinct for it."

For one evening, a coach questioned whether getting the best really paid off. Phil Buck was coaching at Frankfort and had a good team. The young coach listened and took the advice of veteran Coach Marion Crawley when he said, "If you want to be successful as a coach, hire the best referees." Let Buck tell the rest:

"I got McBride and Hilligoss for the Frankfort-Indianapolis Tech game, the most important outing of the year for us. From the opening tip-off, our boys were in trouble. By halftime, we were in foul trouble and I was saying to myself, I thought we hired the best referees but now I am wondering.

"By the time the game ended, Tech had clobbered us by twenty points and I lost my job.

"But, getting fired at Frankfort turned out to be the biggest break of my coaching career. I got the Madison Heights job and the rest is history." Buck stayed there until retiring from coaching.

It was amazing how well dressed a coach could look prior to the start of a game, and how disheveled he became by the time it ended. None epitomized this more than Steve Lemley, coach at Straughn in Henry County. You would have thought Lemley was working for a fashion magazine before the game, dark suit, white shirt, matching tie and even a handkerchief in his coat pocket.

By the end of the first quarter, the coat was gone and the tie unloosened. When halftime rolled around, the tie was gone. By the end of the third quarter, the shirt sleeves were rolled up and his shirttail was hanging out.

As each game ended, no matter whether it had been close or not, Lemley was a total wreck.

He told McBride, "If you worked as hard at refereeing as I do at coaching, you would have to shower twice before you head for home."

"I'll take the ball son," Referee Don Snedeker says to a Broad Ripple
player in the 1980 state championship game against New Albany.
Snedeker's officiating partner was Troy Ingram. Broad Ripple won,
73-66.

     -Photo courtsey Don Snedeker

Referee Troy Ingram sees the hand-in-the-face violation in this 1981 state tournament match-up between Shenandoah and Vincennes. The shot did not count on the continuing play and a foul was called on the Shenandoah shooter.
     -Photo courtsey Indiana Basketball Hall of Fame

If Referee Dave Habegger had looked to his right, he would have seen Richmond Coach Dick Baumgartner on the playing floor, a violation. The game was at Civic Hall in Richmond in 1969.
     -Richmond Palladium-Item *photo*

Referee Jim Frey has his eyes glued to the battle under the boards in this late sixties sectional contest in Wayne County.
    -Richmond Palladium-Item *photo*

The second half of the 1974 Lawrenceburg against Madison game gets under way as Referee John Thomas tosses the ball high into the air for the jump. Under today's rules, there is no second half jump. Instead, an alternating possession rule allows the ball to be tossed in at the center line. This was the last game Thomas worked before retiring.
    -Photo courtesy John Thomas

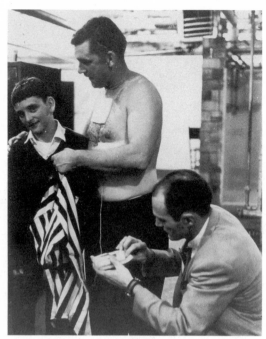

Testing equipment to monitor the heart was attached by Dr. Holland to Referee Danny Jacobs prior to a tournament game at Butler Fieldhouse as son Randy Jacobs looked on.
-Photo courtesy Danny Jacobs

Official Lowell Smith looks for illegal contact as a South Bend Adams player goes up for a shot against New Albany in the 1973 state finals. The Palmyra referee worked the game with Gene Marks.
-Photo courtsey Lowell Smith

Referee Bob Beeson readies to untangle players as a foul occurs under the basket on a put-back shot.
-Richmond Palladium-Item photo

Bill May was in command when he worked the state tournament afternoon game in 1973 at the Indiana University Fieldhouse in Bloomington.

6

A Surprise for Jay McCreary

McBride and Hilligoss had worked together for so many years, most all the coaches in the state knew them by sight. But oh the surprise when a second John Hilligoss appeared on the scene.

During the days of the VanArsdale twins, Indianapolis Manual intended to send a contract to John Hilligoss at Richmond for the Indianapolis Washington game. Instead, it was sent to John Hilligoss at New Albany. Manual Coach Dick Cummins was such a fine gentleman that he refused to rescind the contract when he found out about it, even though he knew the New Albany referee was a rookie at the job.

Cummins contacted McBride and told him of the mistake.

He ask him to explain to his partner the mix-up, then added, "Don, I hate to do this to you on such a big game, but I know you can carry this young man, so give it your best shot."

Near the end of the B-team game, McBride walked into the gymnasium and the first person he saw was Jay McCreary, former Muncie Central coach and now coach at Louisiana State. They exchanged greetings and chatted for a few minutes when McCreary asked, "Who is working with you tonight?"

"Hilligoss."

"When he gets dressed, tell him to come out, I'd like to say hello to him."

McBride, knowing that McCreary was known to tip the bottle on occasion, headed to the dressing room. He found the other referee ready so he said, "Come on out, I have someone I want you to meet."

Now, the John Hilligoss from New Albany looked nothing like the John Hilligoss from Richmond. In addition, he had a southern accent you could cut with a band saw.

"Jay," said McBride, "I want you to meet my partner for the game."

"Oh," said McCreary, puzzled. "What is your name?"

"I'mmm John Hilliegoss," answered the referee.

"Oh come on, I know John Hilligoss and you are not him," said McCreary.

"Yes sir, ah am," answered the referee. "I'mmm John Hilliegoss."

McCreary looked at McBride and said, "Don, I swear, I'll never touch another drop."

Overtime games were not unusual but nine overtimes? It remains an Indiana record and happened this way:

It was the 1964 regional at Marion, in the old coliseum, and the game pitted favored Liberty Center against Swayzee. Bill May and John Thomas called the afternoon game.

Center Coach Richard Butt had an all-star player in Dick Harris and few gave Swayzee a chance. But Swayzee Coach Dave Huffman had an ace up his sleeve and played a controlled game.

Liberty Center led throughout but Swayzee stayed close, and with a minute to play, Harris fouled out. In moments, Swayzee tied the score and a shot at the buzzer missed, overtime.

Even with Harris gone, Liberty Center had a much bigger center than Swayzee and controlled the tip. Coach Butt decided to hold the ball for one shot . . . but missed. Second overtime.

In fact, this scenario was repeated during three more overtimes before both teams took shots and scored in the fifth extra session. But the last shot by Center missed, sixth overtime.

Again the tip to Liberty Center. Again a last shot attempt. In fact, this pattern was repeated in two more extra sessions.

Finally, in the ninth overtime, Swayzee stole the ball for a score and by the time the buzzer sounded to end the marathon, the upset had occurred, Liberty Center was defeated.

"Bluffton Principal Fred Park took care of both referees during that extra hour," said May. "With no action on the floor, we simply stood in one spot. Park gave us popcorn to eat, a Coke to sip and a towel to dry off with. We did not think that game would ever end."

"I know one thing," added Thomas. "My cows were sure glad when it ended for they were bawling like crazy when I got home." You will find a sign at each end of Swayzee that lets all know who won that marathon game.

Bill May also was involved in one of the wildest two points any team could ever score. It was the Milan sectional, and May was working with Don Call. Jac-Cen-Del and Sunman were going at it full steam when a Jac-Cen-Del player shot and missed with only seconds left to play. Sunman got the rebound and the player threw the ball long down court. It hit the tip of the Sunman receiver's hands and headed out of bounds. But before it got there, another Sunman player leaped into the air and batted it back over his head, ending on his back in the second row of the bleachers.

The ball went high in the air and as a Jac-Cen-Del player spun around, the ball hit him on the right knee and bounced to a teammate who grabbed it, saw one of his buddies open at mid-court and threw it to him. The Jac-Cen-Del forward drove under for two points as the buzzer sounded.

"I was the out official," said May, "and since the ball was going all over the place, I was in a perfect position at mid-court to follow the boy who scored and knew it cleared his hand before the buzzer. There was no argument from Sunman Coach Ken Dieselberg.

"After the game, Jac-Cen-Del Coach Dave Porter laughingly said, "Game plan all the way."

Danny Jacobs was involved in an unusual play at Anderson, and it figured in a win for the Indians. The game was with Madison Heights and it was close all the way. Late in the third quarter, Anderson grabbed a rebound, headed down the floor on a fast break, and the big center turned on the right side of the keyhole for a pass. But the throw was high and to his left.

"I was cutting under the basket from the right to cover the play," said Jacobs, "when I saw the ball coming right at me. I tried to get out of the way, but it was impossible. The ball hit my heel, in bounds, bounced up into the hands of the Anderson center, and he laid it in for two points.

"There was nothing I could do but signal the basket since the ball is in play if it hits a referee, as long as the referee is on the playing floor. Anderson won by two points.

"After the game, Anderson Coach Ick Osborne came to the dressing room, shook my hand and said, 'Danny, you're the best player I got.'"

A referee must always be ready for the unexpected and Danny was a master when confronted with an unusual situation. He said: "I had a game at Gosport in Owen County and the early calls had been going against the host team. The ball went out of bounds near the officials bench and directly in front of the Gosport cheering section. Suddenly, something hit me in the side of the neck and fell to the floor. I looked down and realized it was a Clark Bar. So, I reached down, picked it up, peeled back the paper, took a big bite, stuck the rest in my pocket, and did not have one ounce of trouble the rest of the way."

On occasion, there is a referee-coach combination that simply will not work. No matter how hard a referee tries, it never is good enough. Bill May was working the Madison Heights at Summitville game and the host Coach Jim

Stone was on the referee from the word go. After the game ended, and Summitville lost, he again read the riot act to May, saying he was incompetent.

Stone did not hire May back to referee, but two years later the official was hired to work at another school and the opponent that night was Summitville.

Late in the third quarter, with Summitville again getting beat, a loose ball bounced into Coach Stone's hands and May hurried over to retrieve it. As Stone handed him the ball he said, "You haven't improved one bit."

May answered, "By the looks of the score, you haven't either."

Cooperation between the referees and coaches often made the difference between a bad situation and one both the teams and fans could live with.

Scoop Campbell was officiating a rough-and-tumble game between Kokomo and Anderson in 1961, and the two centers, Mock for the Indians and Ligon for the Kats, had been at each other all evening.

Kokomo Coach Joe Platt loved the run and gun game and had the team to do it. A rebound at the Anderson end came off to Ligon, and his outlet pass started a Kokomo fast break. Campbell was the out official, so down the floor he went full speed, trying to stay ahead of the play. Kokomo scored. But when the referee looked at the other end of the gymnasium, Mock was slowly getting up off the floor.

"I did not know what happened," said Campbell, "but it was obvious that Ligon had decked Mock. I went to Platt and told him I did not see the play, but asked he take Ligon out for the remainder of the game if Anderson Coach Ray Estes would do the same with Mock. Both agreed, order was restored and the game ended without incident. But it was touchy."

One of Campbell's big detractors on the floor was Charlie Maas at Indianapolis Tech. The referee called the fifth foul on Tech star Mel Garland, and out came the coach ranting and raving. Campbell let him have his say and then put a technical on him. Tension remained between the two for a long period of time.

But after both had retired, the two men were paired in a state golf tourney at Kokomo. That night, Maas told the audience, "You know, Scoop refereed many times for me and I often wondered whether he could see very well. Today he found my ball so many times, I must have been wrong."

Martinsville was playing at Connersville and McBride and Hilligoss had the game. A few minutes before it was to start, the overhead light in one corner of the gymnasium went out, making it rather dim. McBride checked with a janitor, and he said it would take him ten minutes or so to locate a bulb and another ten to put it in. Ken Gunning, the Connersville coach, wanted to delay the game since his team would be shooting at that end, but McBride said no, and prepared to toss up the ball.

"Don," screamed Gunning, "my boys won't be able to see the basket."

"Just calm down," said McBride, "the janitor is getting a bulb and we will fix it when he gets back." The game, under the protest of Gunning, started, and the first three trips down the floor, the same Connersville forward canned three from the corner, all dead center. A few minutes later, McBride saw the janitor come into the entrance of the gym, carrying the huge bulb. So he whistled an official's time out.

"What's that for?" screamed Gunning. "Let them play. Let them play."

"Ken," said McBride, "you hollered like a banshee before the game and now we are going to fix it."

It did take ten minutes to complete before play resumed. And the first time down the floor, the same Connersville forward that had hit three in a row in the dark . . . missed his first shot.

Many games were worked by referees when they were ill or in physical pain and few fans ever knew the difference. It was not true in the Bluffton sectional when Bill May could not hide his discomfort. Fans knew there was something wrong but they did not know what. May seemed to be in intense pain and ran bent forward like he was carrying a weight around his neck.

Earlier in the week, May, McBride and Bob Henne got together to discuss the tourney they were to work. As they were getting ready to leave, May picked up three cases of empty Coke bottles in McBride's kitchen and carried them out to his car to take them back to a grocery.

The next morning he could barely get out of bed due to his back being stiff and shooting pains down his leg. Throughout the week, he did everything possible to get back in shape and by the time the tourney started, was feeling better.

He got through the first night without a major problem, but on the second night, just before the end of the first quarter, he was running down the floor when it felt as if someone had hit him in the back with a brick. Time-out was called and it was several seconds before he was able to continue.

At halftime, he sat down in a chair to rest and couldn't get up. McBride and Henne helped him to his feet and urged him to call it quits, saying they could finish the tourney. But May was determined to do his part and he finished that night and the next day without sitting down once during play.

Afterward, McBride, in a great show of sympathy, said, "It was the only time I ever refereed with a hunchback!"

With all the miles referees drove to get to games, it is surprising they did not receive more driving violations tickets than they did.

Frank Sanders and Merle Shively were heading home after working a game at Wakarusa that had gone to overtime. They were tired and it was late, so Sanders was hurrying. At the edge of town, there were Christmas lights in front of a commercial building and Sanders did not see the red stoplight as it blended into the row of lights. When he realized it was red, it was too late and he went on through.

A city policeman was parked in the driveway of a nearby lot and in moments had the two referees stopped. When he walked up to the car, he said: "Hey fella, didn't you see that red light back there?"

Before Sanders could answer, the policeman leaned into the window and realized who the two men were. "Oh, it's you two," he said. "I was at the game and I know neither one of you can see worth a darn. Go home." With that, the policeman turned and walked away.

Basketball fans are fickle. If one of their own players gets hurt, the gymnasium goes as quiet as a mouse. If one of the opponents goes down, the crowd yells, "He deserves it . . . been playin' dirty all night." But a referee . . . ?

Sanders was working the Marion regional and as he went to signal a ball out of bounds, he threw his shoulder out of place. Time was called and the trainer went with him to the dressing room to work on it. The game was held up for some ten minutes.

Expecting a little sympathy from the crowd, as it had been announced that he was injured, Sanders returned to the floor to loud boos and shouts of, "You ain't worked hard enough to hurt yourself." "Come on, play ball. We ain't got all night." Said the referee, "Even the two coaches, Woody Weir and Bill Green, thought I held up the game too long. You just can't win."

Sanders, like many other referees of the time, commented on how some of the small school gymnasiums were great to work in. Roann was one of these, with an excellent small floor and good facilities for showering and dressing.

"On the other hand," said the referee, "at schools like Chili, you dressed in the grade school building and ran across open ground to the gymnasium. When it was below zero, it was mighty cold. Also, Chili only had one shower, so we generally dried ourselves off, put on our street clothes and headed home to shower."

This was not true of the bigger schools, where facilities were of the best, but the problems of a game were the same.

The referee's decision is final and there is no way he is going to change it, especially after the game is over.

Scoop Campbell was working with Ernie Baldwin in an early season game between Jeffersonville and a team from Louisville, Kentucky. The Louisville team was 7-0 and thought the game would be a warm-up for its conference season. But it did not turn out that way.

From the opening tipoff, Campbell said Jeffersonville gave the much bigger Louisville team all it wanted. The game was rough and several fouls were called. Twice near fights started, but were stopped before action had to be taken. With a minute to go, Louisville scored, giving it a four point lead. But as the teams came down the floor, a Louisville player gave a Jeffersonville opponent an elbow and a fight broke out. Fans poured onto the floor, policemen raced into the melee, and when order was restored, Campbell threw both players off the floor.

Jeffersonville took the ball out and as time ran out, scored, but still lost by two points.

In the dressing room afterward, the official scorekeeper said, "Scoop, we got a problem."

"Oh," said the referee, "what's that?"

"The boy who scored the final basket was one of the two you tossed off the floor. He didn't go."

"Tell you what," said Campbell. "That last basket is going to count, right boy or not. This game is over, so forget it." The scorekeeper shrugged his shoulders, walked out, and no more was heard about the mixup.

Senior referees were always playing jokes on junior referees and Campbell was the target of one of these by Hilligoss. The game was at Losantville in Randolph County, and as the Star Spangled Banner was being sung, Hilligoss whispered to Campbell, "Scoop, did you get the game ball?"

"I thought you did," Campbell whispered back.

The song ended and the crowd roared and Campbell yelled at Hilligoss, "I'll go back and get it."

He rushed to the dressing room but there was no ball in sight. After a quick check, Campbell dashed back to the gymnasium in time to see Hilligoss leaning over the scorer's bench and getting the ball he had hidden there before the National Anthem.

In later years, Campbell became the tormentor and enjoyed every minute of it. "It was a regional game at Fort Wayne," said Campbell, "and I teamed up with Frank Carnes to get one on fellow referee Oscar Samuels.

"We were getting ready for the game when Oscar stripped down to his shorts. He was wearing a pair of satin briefs his wife had given him for Valentine's day and they were covered with bright red hearts and cupids."

"Eat your heart out," said the referee, taking it all in stride.

Carnes made sure he was the last one to leave the dressing room and he stuck the shorts in his pocket. He was the referee not working the first afternoon game, so he sat at the end of press row, directly across from the main television camera.

Samuels tossed the ball up for the opening jump and headed down court. As he returned his face suddenly got as red as the hearts and cupids, for there, draped over the end of the scorer's bench for all the world to see, were his Valentine shorts. And the announcer made sure all knew they belonged to the senior official on the floor.

In a split second, a referee must make a decision and if it is wrong, it can cost a team a victory. But these calls must be made and if they end up being wrong, it stands. Campbell had the sectional at Butler Fieldhouse with Ben Davis and Indianapolis Cathedral the top teams. The game was close all the way, and on the final play, a Ben Davis player fired from near center court. Campbell lifted his arms to indicate the ball was in the air before the buzzer sounded, and it hit dead center. Ben Davis advanced. Cathedral was defeated.

"I was sure the ball was in the air before the buzzer," said the referee. "That is, I was sure until the official timer came to the dressing room afterward and told me I blew it. The buzzer sounded as the shooter was starting his motion. In the roar of the crowd, I missed it.

"Oddly enough," said Campbell, "Cathedral Coach Marion Fine did not protest the call."

The old adage of two wrongs do not make a right holds true in refereeing. Bill Larkin was working with Campbell on the Marion game at Wabash in the late fifties. Campbell tossed the ball up for the opening jump, and the tip went to a Wabash player who broke for the goal. But before he got there, the official bench horn sounded and Campbell blew his whistle, stopping the game. The player hit the lay-up but the official ruled it did not count.

At halftime the athletic director of Wabash came to the dressing room and informed the referees that he was going to file a complaint with the IHSAA about a wrong decision on that opening play.

Campbell wrote his letter to the IHSAA office, explaining his position, and waited on the return letter from Commissioner Phillips. It said:

Two wrongs do not make a right. First, the referee should not have blown his whistle until the play was completed. Second, after he blew it, he was right in not counting the basket. The ball was dead the moment the whistle blew. Counting it would not have made the quick blowing of the whistle right.

And, as usual, when Phillips spoke, coaches and referees alike, listened.

The latitude officials had during the Golden Age was unbelievable in comparison with today. If a referee tried this tactic against a fan now, he would be barred from the game. But McBride actually called a game from the bleachers for a full two minutes.

Union City was playing at Winchester and it always meant blood. Hilligoss was working the game with McBride and they had kept it well under control. But there was a problem. A Winchester fan was on McBride from the opening whistle. You could hear his voice throughout the gymnasium on every call that went against his beloved Yellow Jackets.

At halftime, a reporter remarked about "foghorn" in the officials dressing room and McBride said, "Yeh, I know John West from his playing days. I'll shut him up."

The third quarter started and with some two minutes gone, McBride called a foul on a Winchester player and West let him have it full blast. The referee turned toward the bench and started blowing his whistle and kept blowing it as he passed the bench and headed up into the crowd. West saw him coming and started to move out. "Hold it, John," yelled McBride. "Sit down. If you can see the game better from here than I can on the floor, then I'll call it from here."

He sat down next to the fan and for the next two minutes, called the game from his seat while Hilligoss worked the floor. Action stopped and everyone in the gymnasium went totally silent as McBride stood up. "Hell, John," he said, "you can't see any better here than I can out there," and he returned to the floor. It did the job. West was as quiet as a mouse.

McBride and Hilligoss proved that it is impossible to please both the coaches and the fans. Call too many fouls and the fans are all over you. Don't call the fouls and the coaches wonder whether you should be paid or not.

The 1949 Madison-Evansville Bosse game at Evansville was certain to be rugged as both had top rated teams. When McBride and Hilligoss went to the floor for pre-game preliminaries, the crowd got on them full force.

"Keep your whistle in your pocket and let them play," yelled one fan.

"Whistle-happy McBride," yelled another one.

As the two teams lined up for the tipoff, McBride whispered to Hilligoss, "This crowd needs a lesson. Let them play. Call only the most flagrant fouls."

That is what they did. Only thirteen fouls were called total for the evening. Madison Coach Ray Eddy came into the dressing room after the game and asked, "What's wrong with you two? I can't believe you called only thirteen fouls."

"The crowd wanted to see them play, so we let them play," said McBride.

"Yeh, the crowd loved it," answered Eddy, "but I'm not so sure the kids did. I know I didn't. We lost."

There was a time when it was not unusual for a new rule to suddenly crop up as sectionals were ready to begin. Often it would concern something that seemingly had caused problems all season. Seldom did it work and referees hated the change. This one in the early forties said that a player must not touch the ball after it goes through the hoop, until the referee handles it.

Gene McNutt was working with McBride at the Aurora sectional. Before the game, Dutch Schmidt, the Aurora coach, and Red Benedict, Lawrenceburg coach, came into the dressing room.

"We want to make sure you are going to call the new rule after a goal is made," Schmidt told the referees.

"It's in the book so we'll call it," answered McBride. "Just make sure you do," Benedict chimed in.

The game started, Aurora scored the first basket and the player flipped the ball to McNutt, who immediately called a technical. Down the floor they went, the Lawrenceburg player hit the technical and got the ball out of bounds.

On the next play a Lawrenceburg player did exactly the same as the Aurora player earlier and again McNutt called the T. The scenario was repeated.

Two baskets were scored without incident but again an Aurora player tapped the ball to the referee after scoring and McNutt whistled another technical. As McBride took the ball he told McNutt, "It's only a T if it delays the game. Don't call a touch any more or we will be here all night."

Heading back down the floor, McBride hollered to the Aurora coach, "Enough?"

"Enough," he yelled back. The rule was soon removed from the books.

Another rule that did not last long cost Lafayette Jeff a win over Indianapolis Crispus Attucks. It said if a player missed a free throw, he still got a second attempt. Coaches and referees alike hated the rule for it condoned inefficiency.

In the heat of the final moments of the 1952 Jeff-Attucks game, a Lafayette player shot a free throw and it missed everything. McBride grabbed the ball and gave it to an Attucks player out of bounds. Attucks hurried down the floor and scored as time ran out, winning by one point. As McBride was walking off the floor, Sammy Lyboult, assistant coach at Jeff, came up and asked, "Mac, we had another shot on that free throw didn't we?"

"I blew it, Sammy," answered the referee.

The three-point shot was tried out by the IHSAA in the nineteen fifties, long before it became common as it is now. McBride and Dean Malaska, Coach Pat Malaska's brother, had the game. Bud Bateman, Lawrenceburg coach, and Harold Petro, coach at Franklin, agreed ahead of time on the experiment. The custodian at Lawrenceburg put temporary tape at the nineteen-foot mark, semi-circling the floor, and the players loved it.

Both coaches and both referees were instructed to send letters to the IHSAA after the game, giving good and bad points.

There also were two IHSAA officials in the stands. Although all four letters recommended the three-point line be established, it was 1987 before it was adopted.

One of the major gripes from referees concerning sports writers stems from the fact few ever attend referee clinics or study the rule book.

"They write what they see," said McBride, "but if they do not know the rules, mistakes can be made. There is nothing that irritates a referee more than to be right on a call and get criticized in the newspaper the next day."

"During the Golden Age," said the Richmond referee, "we had some excellent sports writers and some who were not so good. There were men like Bob Barnet of the *Muncie Star*, Bob Collins of *The Indianpolis Star*, Bob Ford at Kokomo, Jimmy Angelopolous from the *Indianapolis Times*, Red Haven over at Anderson and two from the Richmond *Palladium-Item*, Ken Murphy and my younger brother, Cy McBride, who always gave us a fair shake.

"Then there were some who liked to take a poke at a referee, especially if the writer thought the official was from some hick town and had no business being in the big time."

"They knew the rules and fundamentals of basketball, and it was a delight to work with them."

Jack O'Neal, an Indianapolis referee, had the Indianapolis regional with McBride and brought Bill Fox with him. Fox was sports editor for the *Indianapolis News* and daily carried a column called, "The Foxes Den." He was well known to have a poison pen.

Sure enough, in the next issue, prior to the regional finals, Fox took a swipe at McBride, accusing him of using signals to the scorer's bench that could not be understood. His column made it appear O'Neal had to carry McBride in the game and that the Richmond official did a poor job.

When McBride walked onto the floor for the championship game, he spotted Fox and went over to him.

"Mr. Fox," he said, "I read your column. Did you ever hear the bench ask me what I meant by my signals or what was going on?"

Fox answered, "No."

"That," said the official, "is all I worry about. I do not care whether you get my signals or not, Mr. Fox, only that the bench gets them." With that, McBride walked away.

A year later, the Richmond official had the Lafayette

regional with O'Neal and again the Indianapolis referee brought Fox with him. "Don," he said, "do you know Bill Fox?"

"Oh, sure," answered McBride, "I remember him. He writes for *The Indianapolis Star.*" Fox said, "No, no. I write for *The Indianapolis News.*"

"Oh," countered McBride, "I wouldn't know about that. We hicks don't get the *News* over at Richmond, only the *Star.*"

Fox looked at the referee, paused and then said, "Tell you what McBride. You get off my case and I'll get off yours."

"Fair enough," answered the referee, and Fox never wrote another negative line about McBride, although he saw him work several games, including two state finals.

Referees, like many coaches, were well known for patting themselves on the back. But for the official, it was a necessity. You got a sectional if you pleased enough coaches to get recommended. You moved on up the ladder by performance and if no one else bragged about your officiating, then you did it yourself.

Bob Fisher pulled the ultimate con on his fellow officials. He asked Homer Owens what help he could give him before his first regional game. The veteran referee told him to call this game the same as any other, and once it started, he would forget the pressure.

Fisher did work a good game, and when the referees returned to their motel between the afternoon and evening sessions, Fisher was the last one to enter the door. As he started to close it, he said to someone in the parking lot, "What did you say? Well, thank you, sir. Yes, that was my first regional game. I did my best. I wanted to look good."

Fisher closed the door and Owens ask, "Who was that?"

"I don't know," answered the referee, "but he must have liked my work in the tourney." "Sure is nice to get compliments," Owens said, "especially in your first regional game."

It was several months later, Fisher confessed to Owens,

"I made the whole thing up. There was no one in the parking lot. Sure sounded good though, didn't it?"

Referees expect the people sitting at the official bench to quietly do their jobs without rooting for either team. But it did not always work out that way.

In a game at Arlington, the official scorer kept waving his arms and disagreeing on calls made by Owens and Charlie Northam. Finally, Owens had enough, so he went to the bench and asked, "Sir, are you enjoying your position here at the scorer's table?"

"I most certainly am," replied the scorer.

"Then," said the referee, "you keep score and quit refereeing or we will get someone else to do your job and you can go up in the stands with the rest of the radicals."

At the next time out, Northam came over to Owens and asked, "Do you know who that scorer is?"

"No," answered his partner, "and to tell you the truth, I don't care."

"Okay," said Northam, walking away, "I just thought you might like to know he is the chairman of the IHSAA board of control."

Pounding the floor night after night took a tremendous toll on the legs of the referees. They sought out different liniments, hot packs, cold packs and even "miracle" creams, seldom with much success.

In order to keep better circulation in his legs, McBride would put on long nylon hose while riding to a game. Hilligoss conned him into rubbing his legs with a new liniment he said he was using, guaranteeing it would help circulation.

As McBride started sweating, once the game got underway, his legs got hotter and hotter. At the end of the quarter he said to his partner, "What did you give me? My legs are on fire."

"Maybe you're allergic to it," answered Hilligoss, with an innocent face. "Get in the shower at halftime and wash it off with hot water."

From Broadcloth To Jersey

In the early days of officiating, all referees wore broad-cloth shirts. Most were a putrid green color, but they did not have to be that color. McBride said that by halftime, these sad shirts looked like they'd been slept in. Some of the referees, like Maurice Criswell, would change shirts at halftime, but many others simply did not have the luxury of two shirts. The clothing worn by a referee has changed dramatically over the years.

The earliest uniforms were long sleeved, broadcloth dresstype shirts, with buttons down the front and generally of a neutral color. Pants could be any color and often two referees on the floor would have on different colored trousers. These pants were wool and extremely hot to wear. Shoes generally were black in color and had canvas sides.

In the early thirties, striped black and white shirts were introduced, but still of broadcloth material. Not only were they hot, but by halftime they were wrinkled and showed sweat stains. It was required that the pants be gray in color. Although it was not mandatory to wear this outfit during the season, it was required for tournaments. Many referees could not afford the striped shirts so if you had two, you shared.

In the spring of 1946, Don McBride had the Muncie sectional with Frank Sanders and Fred White. He had been so miserable in the broadcloth shirts that he purchased a football referee jersey, had his wife cut off the sleeves and wore it at the tournament. The football jersey had wider stripes than the broadcloth basketball shirt, resulting in Commissioner L.V. Phillips making a rule that all referees must wear the same style shirt. Phillips also decreed nothing but long sleeved shirts would be worn.

In the fall of 1946, the jersey was adopted because of its easy-care factor. The jersey could be worn throughout an entire tournament without showing a wrinkle, if you could not afford more than one shirt. Soon after, dark trousers were adopted and black shoes were mandatory.

It was twelve years later before the wearing of short sleeve shirts was allowed. The only rule was, both referees on the floor must wear the same sleeve length shirt. In tournaments, only long sleeves could be worn.

McBride tried it, and only realized as they were called to start the second half, that Hilligoss had conned him again. When he got hold of the bottle it read, *To remove, use cold water only. Hot water may cause excessive burning.*

"I never did get even with John for that one," laughed McBride.

Rowdy fans are a problem. But when that number grows to fifteen thousand rowdy fans, what do you do?

Oscar Samuels was senior official at the Fort Wayne sectional. From the opening whistle, the fans were all over him. No matter what he called, it was wrong, and on several occasions, things were thrown onto the floor. Finally the official had enough.

He stopped the game, went to the announcer, picked up the microphone and said, "If you do not settle down, or if there is one more thing thrown on this floor, I am going to clear this fieldhouse and we will finish this game in silence."

It worked. There were no more interruptions and nothing else came flying out of the stands. In the dressing room after the game, Samuels said to McBride, who was there as a spectator on an off day from his sectional at Churubusco, "Could I do that? Could I have cleared the fieldhouse?"

"Oscar," said the Richmond official. "This fieldhouse is huge. It must hold 15,000 people. It would have taken you until midnight to get them all outside. My advice . . . just ignore them." Oscar said it was good advice and he never let the fans get to him again.

It was important that officials never get too big for their britches and there were coaches who made sure they did not.

Coach Bob Warner saw McBride the week after he refereed the 1951 state finals. "Hey McBride," he called, "I got a class tourney Saturday at Williamsburg and I want you and Hilligoss to referee for me."

"Sure," answered the Richmond official. "We'll be there."

"Nah," said Warner, "I was only kidding. You just worked the state and I know you got better things to do than work a class tournament."

"So!" McBride answered.

"You mean you actually will come?" said Warner. "Well, I'll be damned. Okay, I'll count on it." And as an after-thought he added, "I got another surprise for you. You both are going to sell Cokes at halftime and I have aprons for you to wear."

The two referees did work the tournament and they did sell Cokes, and the kids and fans loved it.

Rules Constantly Changing

Rules constantly were being changed. Some changes were for the good while others were plain foolishness. In 1929 a rule, still in effect, set the circumference of a basketball at 29 1/2 inches. This makes the diameter of the ball nine inches. The diameter of a goal is eighteen inches. This means two basketballs can be put through a goal side by side.

In 1948 a new rule said a player must hold his hand up to admit he created a foul. If a player was loaded with fouls, a teammate would hold up his hand and in many cases got by with it. This foolish rule lasted until 1974, when it was dropped.

In 1956 a new rule said no player could hang on the rim after hitting a shot. In 1984 it was decided it was better for a shooter who had dunked the ball to grab the rim and hang on rather than come down on top of a player and cause an injury.

In 1957 a new rule said that a player who has legal contact with the ball may continue play while the ball is in the cylinder. Dunking now was legal without using the word. But the 1956 rule remained that a player could not touch the rim or basket while taking a shot. That rule still is in effect today. The reality is a player slamming a ball through the basket cannot do it without hitting the rim. Golden Age referees agree, technically every dunk today is a violation.

In 1967 a new rule said dunking during a game is illegal. This actually penalized the big man under the basket, as did the widening of the free throw lanes from six to twelve feet in 1957. In 1970 dunking a ball during warm-ups before a game or at halftime was ruled illegal. In 1976 the rule again was changed to allow players to dunk the ball during a game but not in practice before a game or at intermission. To Golden Age referees, the dunking rule is called the "showboat rule."

The year 1963 saw a rule that a game could not be stopped while a player tied his shoe. In the closing seconds, when a coach tried to get his bench players into the game, often a referee would stop the game himself . . . to tie his shoe.

7

The Big "O" Was The Best

Attucks was playing at Indianapolis Cathedral and Coach Pete Wyngold had his players keying on Oscar Robertson. By halftime, Oscar was in foul trouble and had scored only eight points.

As Homer Owens and his partner, Charlie Northam, were returning to the floor for the second half, Attucks Coach Ray Crowe fell into step with them. "I got a boy out there trying to do three men's jobs and he is only seventeen years old. He is trying to coach, trying to referee and trying to play, and I do not know whether he can do any of them right tonight."

As the two teams lined up for the second half jump, Owens asked the two captains, "Are you ready?"

Oscar leaned down and said, "Yes, sir. Mr. Crowe over there is going to coach . . . you and Mr. Northam are going to referee . . . and I am going to play ball."

Robertson, the best according to Owens, scored twenty-six points the second half and Attucks won going away. That was the year, 1956, when Attucks finished undefeated, winning the state title over Lafayette Jeff, 79 to 57. Oscar ended his high school career with thirty-nine points in the championship game.

Oscar also was the best player McBride ever saw play in a game he officiated. "Oscar was all business," said the referee. "He was so intense every moment, for there was no horse play. Oscar simply gave it 110 percent the entire game. He was the best."

Northam and Owens saw this proven on another occasion as they called a game between Attucks and Tech. At halftime, Oscar had four fouls. They learned later that Coach Ray Crowe chewed his star up one side and down the other in the dressing room, telling him to cut out the rough stuff and play his style of ball. Oscar played the entire second half without committing his fifth foul.

"The outstanding players come to the top," added Glen Wisler, "and Robertson took a back seat to no one.

"I worked the Indianapolis sectional," he continued, "the year Attucks was headed for its undefeated season and state title. They had clobbered Beech Grove, 91-30; Howe, 72-58 and Cathedral, 57-49. Now they were in the championship game against Shortridge, and things were not going so good. No one on Attucks was playing up to par, and the fans were getting rowdy.

"On an Attucks fast break," he said, "there was one of those blocking or charging fouls that often are determined by a split second, and I called charging on Attucks. The crowd went wild, screaming for my head. I looked over at the bench and Attucks Coach Ray Crowe was calmly sitting there.

"As we went down the floor for the free throw, I realized someone was trotting up behind me. Then this soft voice said, with a pat on my back, 'Good call, ref.' It was Oscar. What a gentleman. Attucks won, 53-48."

Homer Owens said Lewisville's Marion Pierce was in a class by himself. Coming from a small Henry County school, Pierce in 1961 set the state four year, total-point scoring record, not broken until Damon Bailey accomplished the feat in 1991 at Bedford North Lawrence.

It was the final game of the New Castle sectional and the host school was in a desperate battle with Lewisville. With a minute to go, Pierce was fouled and stepped to the free throw line. Owens was ready to hand him the ball when he noticed scratches all over Pierce's shoulders and arms, proof of the battering he had taken under the bucket.

The referee said, "Son, I appreciate your attitude during the ball game." He grinned, pointed over his shoulder and said, "Look at the scoreboard." Lewisville was ahead by six points and held on to win its only sectional title.

In the regional, Pierce played the greatest game of his career in a losing cause. Muncie Central surrounded the Lewisville center with three players and Pierce still scored twenty-five points.

Cecil Tague, while coaching at Spiceland, worked out a sure-fire way of stopping Pierce and beating Lewisville. He decided to triple team the scoring wizard, keeping him away from those easy lay-ups under the basket.

"In one degree, it worked," said Tague. "We did edge Lewisville in what many called an upset. But in the second degree, my strategy was not so good. Marion scored fifty-six points."

Often a referee found the assistant coach much harder to deal with than the regular coach. Different methods were used to handle these situations.

Charlie Maas, while serving as an assistant coach at Indianapolis Tech, got in trouble with McBride. In a 1953 game, Tech was at Frankfort and the Indianapolis team revolved around its legendary player, Joe Sexson. Late in the third quarter, Sexson, who later coached at Butler University, was camped in the keyhole and simply went to sleep on the amount of time he stood there.

This is one call referees hate to make and often give it a long count instead of the three seconds the rule requires. But after a count of six, McBride blew his whistle and made the call. Maas, thinking the referee had called traveling on the guard holding the ball, yelled, "How could he travel, Mac, he wasn't even dribbling the ball."

McBride said, "Charlie, you do not know what you are talking about and it is going to cost you a T. Besides, I do not like assistant coaches hollering at me."

A few years later, Maas was head coach at Tech and when one of his players was injured, McBride motioned

Maas to come out and check on him. As he knelt over the player, Maas looked up and saw his assistant, Jack Bradford, running toward them. "Jack," he yelled, "get off the floor. McBride doesn't like assistant coaches out here. I know from experience." Maas grinned at the referee and said, "Mind like an elephant."

Referee Dee Williams got into a similar situation in a game between New Castle and Lafayette Jeff. Williams called a charge on a New Castle player and as he went toward the scorers bench, Trojan Coach Randy Lawson did not say a word. But, assistant Coach Walter O'Brien really let him have it.

Williams finished giving the call to the official scorer, turned to the New Castle bench and said, "Randy, find a seat six rows up in the crowd for your assistant, and tell him to be quiet." He did and O'Brien watched the remainder of the game as a fan.

Bill Hile was working with Glen Wisler at Lafayette Jeff, in a game with Logansport. They were not having any trouble with Coach Crawley, but his assistant, Sammy Lyboult, was constantly griping about something.

"We took it for awhile," said Wisler, "but at a time-out, Hile said he had had enough. He walked over to the Jeff bench, pointed at Lyboult and said, 'Sammy, I am going to give you two choices. One, you either get out that door and do not come back during this game or two, you go sit in the top row of the bleachers and I mean the top row.'

"Sammy did as he was told and watched the remainder of the game from the top row of the end bleachers," laughed Wisler.

Charlestown Coach Johnny Woods decided he better find a smaller assistant to coach defense, especially if he used him under the opposing team's basket, an illegal maneuver. "They were playing Silver Creek and Jim Patterson had the game with me," said John Thomas. "A foul was called and as we got together at the free throw line, Jim said, 'we got a problem.'

"What's up?" asked Thomas.

"Somebody is under this basket that shouldn't be here," he answered.

"I looked at the bleachers," said the referee, "and there sat the Charlestown assistant, sticking out like a sore thumb. The reason was, he was 6'-5" and stood head and shoulders above anyone else seated there. Jim wiggled his finger at the assistant, grabbed his arm when he stepped onto the floor and marched him the full length to the Charlestown bench. We did not give Charlestown a technical, although we probably should have done so."

Often a referee will try to calm a coach down before a game gets underway, but it does not always work. "I was working the Fort Wayne regional with McBride, Hilligoss and Northam," said Joe Mullins, "when I realized the Auburn coach, Randy Lawson, was a bundle of nerves.

" 'Calm down,' I told him, but he actually was shaking and repeating over and over, 'This is it. This is it. We gotta win. We gotta win.' I realized I could not get through to him and I thought starting the game would help ease his torment. But it did not. He was up and down the entire game, pacing in front of the bench, rubbing his head and only when the game ended with an Auburn victory, did a smile show on his face.

"I did not see his team in the semistate, nor the finals, but if ever there was a coach heading for ulcers, it was Randy."

If they can get by with it, basketball coaches will use every tactic under the sun to get a call their way. Marion Crawley at Lafayette Jeff was a master.

John Thomas and Charlie Stump had the regional at Lafayette and the Crawley-coached team was playing a tough Lebanon ball club, led by the great Rick Mount. Lebanon was having a rather easy time of it for three quarters. In fact, as the fourth period started, people began leaving the gymnasium.

"But, as often happens," said Thomas, "Jeff caught fire and started roaring back. With two minutes to play, Lebanon had allowed Lafayette to get back in the game, down eight points.

"I was the out official when a Jeff player stole the ball at mid-court and made a drive for the basket. But a Lebanon player saw it coming and raced ahead, turning, setting and waiting for the shooter to go up. I also had a jump on the play and was in perfect position to see the Jeff shooter charge full tilt into the defensive player, knocking him end over end.

"I blew the charge, and as I did, the Jeff player hit the floor and could have won an 'Oscar' for his performance. In a second, Crawley was at my side."

"John," he calmly said, "the other official has got it a block." This, of course, would have meant a jump ball at the Jeff end of the floor if one official called it one way and the other official the other way.

Thomas answered, "No, Marion, I did not hear another whistle blow out front, the call stands. Plus, now that you are on the floor, you either must take this 'Oscar' winner out or you get a technical. Take your choice."

Thomas said Crawley threw both hands in the air and said, "John, I guess you can't be pushed."

"You are right," answered the referee. "It is a charge."

Jim Patterson from Fairland was working with Thomas on the Kokomo game at Marion and few could get worked up more than the host team's coach, Woody Weir.

"It was the usual head-banger between these two teams," said Thomas, "and we made a few tough calls along the way, always getting a big protest if it went against Woody.

"Near the end of the third quarter," he continued, "I called a blocking foul against a Marion player, and Woody rushed onto the floor, grabbed the ball out of my hands and threw it halfway to the rafters.

"Woody," I yelled, pointing at him, "if that ball hits the floor, you got a technical. Woody looked up, saw the ball coming down to his right and made a beautiful, diving catch. He tossed me the ball with a grin and went to the bench."

Referees must have a sense of humor or remarks made by coaches would end in far more technicals than were called.

Howard Plough was working a game in Rush County when the captain of the team was injured and had to leave the floor.

After the boy was helped off and play was ready to resume, Plough went to the coach and asked, "Who is to be your captain?" Without missing a beat, the coach answered, "Why don't you guess? You been guessing all evening anyhow."

Plough and Karl Bly had a pleasant experience after a season had ended. The two, by chance, worked the last two games of the season for the Parker Panthers in Randolph County, one at home and one on the road.

Then in the sectional, they were assigned to Farmland, and the schedule had them on games where Parker again played, in fact, three games in a row. This meant the Panthers' final five games were refereed by the same two officials.

After the season ended, Bly, an excellent speaker, was secured by Parker to give the all-sports banquet talk. As it was coming to a close, Parker principal Pop Davidson presented Bly, and Plough, who was not present, with a varsity "P" and a certificate that said, "Certificate of Meritorious Award, Parker High School. This is to certify that Karl Bly (Howard Plough) has been awarded the officiating monogram in basketball for the 1958-59 season." Attached was the purple varsity P. Bly said the fact Parker won the sectional they refereed did not hurt matters one bit.

Cloyce Quakenbush, coach at Fountain City, was a referee baiter, as well as one of the best small-school mentors in the state. The Fountain City gymnasium actually was a stage and was twelve feet short of the minimum seventy-four length required in the fifties. The audience sat in theater seats on one side. The teams also sat off the stage, as did the men at the official's bench.

Bly, a heavyweight, squatted down to better see a play, his back to the jammed audience. As he went back down the floor, Quakenbush grabbed his leg. "Let go," shouted Bly, not looking at the coach. Down the floor came the teams again and again Bly squatted to see a play. This time Quakenbush grabbed both of his legs, holding him fast.

"I blew my whistle, spun around and started to tell the coach I was blowing a T when he yelled, 'Karl, the seat of your pants is ripped out.' I reached back and sure enough, I touched bare behind. I had on a jock strap but no shorts.

"I told Plough, the other referee, to hold the fort, I would be right back. I hurried to the dressing room and put on my suit pants. When I came running back into the gym I received a standing ovation."

Bly also finished a rewarding but tiring night when he refereed both the A and B games by himself. It was Williamsburg at Fountain City, Warner vs. Quakenbush, and this rivalry was one of the best for small schools in the state. It was time for the B-game to start and no second official had arrived. The Fountain City principal checked his files but could not find a contract for the game. Still, he was sure it had been sent and a second official would arrive for the A-game, so he asked Bly to work the first one by himself. He did so without incident.

The referee freshened up in the dressing room between games, but when a second official did not arrive, he walked to the gymnasium floor to talk to the principal.

"Karl," said the principal, "I must not have sent out a contract for this game. I'll tell you what I will do. I will give you a couple more dollars if you will work it by yourself."

"Whoa!" answered the referee. "This is going to cost you thirty bucks or forget it." Quackenbush, standing nearby, and thoroughly disgusted with the principal, yelled, "Get fifty dollars if you can."

Bly called both teams together and told them he would work along the seating section of the stage gymnasium, and would cover from foul line to foul line, no farther.

"I made it through the first half," said the referee, "but near the end of the third quarter, I simply ran out of gas. So, I blew my whistle, turned to the official bench and said, do not start the clock until I say so. I am pooped. I told the coaches to let their players keep warm by shooting if they so desired, but I had to rest.

"I sat on a chair for several minutes before restarting the game. It ended with Fountain City winning, 71-70.

"As I headed for my car, after changing clothes, players from both schools were waiting to shake my hand and I heard a fan say, 'Now that is the way a game should be played. Let the players play.' It made me feel darn good . . . tired, yes, but a happy tired."

Coaches loved to take a good natured poke at referees if the occasion presented itself. Howard Sharpe was one of the best with the needle. His remark, made at a Basketball Hall of Fame dinner in Indianapolis, remains a classic. Said Sharpe, "One nice thing about the future is, if I ever get too blind to coach, I can always become a referee."

There have been many changes in rules through the years, not all of them for the good, nor have all of them stuck. These rules changes are still in effect.

The three-second rule in the free throw lane was put in place in 1936. "This remains one of our poorest rules," said McBride. "with the widening of the free throw lane from six to twelve feet in 1956, it virtually became impossible for a big man to move into the zone and back out in three seconds, unless he did not stop. All referees hate to make this call." The center jump ended in 1937. In 1939 the backboards were moved from two feet to four feet from the end line. The change from four to five fouls and you are out, began in 1944 and the three-point shot was adopted in 1987.

A 1938 Rule Changed Basketball

Referees agree that the most significant rule change that has taken place was the adoption of the ten-second backcourt rule in 1938. "Prior to that time," said McBride, "a player could hold the ball at his end of the court an entire quarter if no defensive player came after him. There were games when a player receiving the ball would place it on the floor and sit down on it until he was challenged. After the new rule went into effect, the team on offense had only ten seconds to cross the center line. If the line was not crossed, the ball went out of bounds to the opposing team. The rule still is in effect."

Following the adoption of the 1938 rule, there was no difficulty in its implementation; floors were simply divided in half with a line across the center. There was no consistency to the size of floors because no rule on size had been endorsed by the rules committee. Most floors were at least forty-two feet wide but the length varied. Some small schools had floors under seventy feet in length while larger courts were as long as eighty-five feet. Today the high school floors are standard at fifty feet wide and eighty-four feet long.

In 1939 a new rule said the minimum court size must be forty-two by seventy-four feet. This was done to standardize the half-court floor length at thirty-seven feet, no matter what the overall length of the floor might be. But some could not meet this requirement without knocking out walls so they simply overlapped the center line. The Fountain City gym, for example, was sixty-four feet long. Measuring thirty-seven feet from the end line meant both of the ten-second lines had to go past the center line, leaving three lines across the middle of the court. The referees called these lines "railroad tracks."

"Confusion reigned," said McBride, "as it was difficult to tell in the heat of a game which line was the right one. This rule was changed in 1967 when the center line became standard as the ten-second line. It remains in effect today."

The most controversial rule, committing an intentional foul, is the one referees decline to call. McBride commented on the reason he believes it is overlooked. "Referees simply do not have the guts to call it. If they did, it would clean up the game tremendously. Something needs to be done."

"I agree," said referee Charlie Fouty, "and I also am tired of watching one high school team knock the hell out of another one and win the game through sheer intimidation. It is my opinion there are several referees today who need to hang it up.

"The problem stems from the fact that college players want the physical contact of the pros and high school players want the physical contact of the colleges. Something must change this or we are going to lose every last shred of the meaning of a well-played game."

Marion Pierce was a good example of a big center who often took a physical beating under the boards without complaining. And when something did upset him, he complained to his coach, Bob Scott, and not to the referees.

"Marion was a natural athlete," said Scott, "but when it came to academics, he left a lot to be desired. I tried my best to make it simple for Marion and then let it sink in."

Lewisville was playing Middletown and both Pierce and the Middletown center, Reedy, were camping in the three-second lane. Early in the second quarter, McBride called the two centers to him and told them to get out of the keyhole or he would start calling a violation. Reedy did so, but Marion still stayed far too long.

At halftime, Scott came to McBride and said, "Marion says you are trying to coach him. What's up?"

"Have you ever explained to him what the keyhole is?" asked McBride. "I am trying to avoid a three-second call."

"Oh," answered Scott, quickly walking away.

McBride said he saw the coach go to his star center, take him to the foul lane and explain what the word keyhole meant. He simply had never been told. It ended the problem.

Talking to a player prior to a game, often ends with a violation's being stopped before it begins. South Bend Central Coach Jimmy Powers came to McBride before the start of his game at Muncie Central against Jay McCreary and the Bearcats.

"Don," he said, "watch Bonham [Muncie's great center Ron Bonham], he backs up in the keyhole and not only does he travel, he charges."

When the referee called the captains to the center of the floor for instructions, he told Bonham, "The coach of South Bend says when you get the ball in the keyhole, you back into the defender and it is a violation. Don't do it."

The Muncie center smiled and said, "Yes, sir, Mr. McBride, I'll watch it."

"That," the Richmond official told his partner in the game, "is called preventive officiating."

One of Kokomo's great players in 1959 was Jimmy Rayl. McBride said that referees hated to work when Rayl played for he had one bad habit. After every whistle against Kokomo, he would question the referee as to why he made the call. Most referees would brush him off and move on, but after this happened on every play the first quarter, Kokomo Coach Joe Platt realized McBride was getting irritated. With one minute gone in the second period, Platt took Rayl out. A few seconds later he was back and did not say one word to the referees the rest of the first half.

Platt came into the dressing room as the second half was ready to start and McBride asked, "What did you tell Rayl?" Platt grinned and said, "I told him to shut up and just play the game. McBride doesn't give a damn who you are and he is going to nail you if you don't cut it out."

When Joe Platt was buried, the two pallbearers who carried the casket across from each other were Rayl and McBride.

Platt was not only a great coach but, although tough when he had to be, also was a favorite of most referees.

As he lay critically ill in a Kokomo hospital, dying of cancer, McBride drove up to see him. When Platt's wife saw him coming, she was surprised and pleased. She told him, "Don, you are welcome to go in, but he won't recognize you."

"I'll take that chance," answered the referee.

McBride said as he approached the bed he saw that Platt had his eyes closed and knew death was not far away. He leaned over the bed and said in a commanding voice, "It's a charge!"

Platt opened his eyes and a faint smile hit his lips as he said, "McBride, what in the hell are you doing here?"

As the official turned away, Platt's wife said, "Don, he knew you. That is his first response in days."

McBride answered, "He knew the word 'charge' for he used to tell me all that he ever heard when I refereed for him was, 'it's a charge.' "

The Richmond referee worked at knowing players by name, thereby making a game much more personal. But it also worked against him on at least one occasion.

Shelbyville's Bill Garrett was an excellent player. His quickness was well known but even McBride was fooled on one play. As Garrett headed down the side on a fast break, an opposing player got position in front of him and McBride whistled a charging foul. The problem was, Garrett somehow twisted in the air and did not touch the other player. McBride had anticipated the call before it happened and now had egg on his face.

"Bill," said the referee, as they went down the floor, "I owe you one."

Knowing McBride had their game the next night and that Shelbyville was comfortably leading this one, Garrett answered, "Save it for tomorrow night. I may need it worse then." The incident taught the Richmond referee never to anticipate, but wait until the play actually unfolds.

Richmond's excellent athletic director Lyman Lyboult was instrumental in Homer Owens working several games for the Red Devils and in him becoming a part of the referee team for the Wayne County Tournament nine years in a row.

Owens said Lyboult was a master at diplomacy and used this incident in the county tournament as an example.

"In the late fifties the IHSAA designated that all goal rims must be painted orange," he said, "but because the tournament was late in the year, paint on the Civic Hall goals had worn off. After his team was on the floor to practice, the Boston coach told Lyboult he wanted the baskets changed to meet the rules. The Richmond athletic director did not bat an eye, he said, 'It will take us some time to get it done, but if you and your opponent are willing to wait, we will change them.'

"Reluctantly the other coach agreed and the tournament was held up while the goals were changed," said Owens.

"But," added the referee, "it didn't do any good. Boston, the tourney favorite, lost the game, and Economy, coached by Bill Townsend, grabbed the title."

Charlie Northam was an excellent referee, calling the plays as they happened and seldom changing speed as he maneuvered the floor.

Southport was playing at Indianapolis Cathedral when Northam called a blocking foul on a Southport player. As he turned to the scorer's bench to give the signal, out on the floor came Coach Jewell Young.

"Jewell," said Northam, "get back to your chair and sit down."

Young ranted and raved as he backed up to the folding chair where he had been seated. But still in a rage, he committed the unpardonable sin against a referee, he reached out and put his hand against Northam's shoulder. Without thinking, Northam put his hand against Young's chest and pushed him back onto the chair. What he didn't expect was, the chair slid on the slick floor, Young missed the seat and ended flat on his back. Northam whistled a T on him and Southport fans screamed for his hide. They never let up the rest of the game, but after it was over, Young walked off the floor with Northam and said, "Sorry about the incident. You did an excellent job tonight."

Jeffersonville was playing Indianapolis Attucks at the Shortridge gymnasium when Northam called a charging foul on a Jeffersonville player. When he turned to signal the call, he saw Jeffersonville Coach Bill Johnson walking down the center of the floor from the other end. Northam walked out to meet him, but before he could say a word, Johnson said, "Charlie, go ahead and put a T on me, but I am going to have my say."

And he did. He informed Northam and referee Bill Findling that they did not know the difference between a charge and a block. Northam pointed to the bench at the other end of the floor and walked with Johnson the entire distance, not saying a word. When he got there, Charlie said, "You done? Okay." He turned to the bench and yelled, "It's a T." Attucks shot and hit the free throw and got the ball out of bounds.

Oddly enough, even coaches who did not care for McBride's showboating hired him back year after year. Von Jameson, the coach at Middletown, had the reputation of being a stern gentleman. He could get blustery with his players and with the referees. McBride's antics often hit the coach the wrong way, but he never marked the Richmond referee off his schedule.

Muncie Burris was at Middletown and it was an excellent game through the first three periods. As the horn sounded to end the quarter, a photographer asked McBride if it would be all right for him to go onto the floor and get a picture of the Middletown yell section for their school annual.

McBride knew it would be impossible to get the shot in the regular time between quarters, so he told the photographer to go ahead and take all the time he needed.

Jameson, seeing the photographer but not knowing what the referee had told him, came hurrying over and said, "Come on, let's get this game going."

"Von," said McBride, "these kids have yelled for you all season and they deserve a few moments of your time to get their picture taken. Now, calm down. We'll play as soon as the photographer is done."

Jameson glared at McBride and muttered, "I don't know why in the world I hire you."

"Von," answered the referee, "you don't have to, you know. And don't let it bother you if you decide not to do so." The Middletown coach walked away shaking his head, the photographer finished shooting, the game resumed, and Jameson continued to hire the Richmond referee.

When McBride saw potential in a young referee, he worked with him, carefully moving him through his rookie stage. Wes Oler was such a rookie in the early forties, and McBride saw great potential in the young man. He scheduled Oler to work with him in the Lawrenceburg-Vevay game. It is customary for referees to change sides as the game progresses, but McBride stayed on the team bench side of the floor and kept the young referee on the other side.

Early in the second quarter, Lawrenceburg Coach Bud Bateman asked McBride about it. "What's up, Mac?" he inquired. "You are not following procedure. I have not seen Oler on my side of the floor all evening."

"No, and you won't," answered the veteran referee. "I'm keeping him as far away from you as possible."

"You can't do that," answered Bateman.

"Bud," McBride said, "I am doing it and I will continue to do it."

"I'll report you to the IHSAA," threatened the coach.

"And I will report you for intimidating the young referees," answered McBride. It ended the conversation. Oddly enough, the referee and coach remained friends through the years and Oler worked several games for Lawrenceburg during his career.

Getting control of a game early was the prime effort of every referee during the Golden Age. None was better at this than McBride and Oler learned another lesson. In the same year, McBride took him to work a game at Brazil. The opponent was Greencastle and both teams had excellent records, meaning it gave promise of being a hard-fought game from the opening whistle.

On the way down, the Richmond referee told Oler how vital it is to get control of a game in the first few minutes. He explained that if you let the situation get away from you at the start, you never get it back. "You'll do a lousy job," he counselled.

When the referees walked onto the floor, McBride saw the two big centers standing near the center of the floor glaring at each other. When they came out to meet with the officials, they did not shake hands, simply brushed past them, still glaring. McBride warned them to take it easy, but knew they did not hear a word he said.

As soon as the game started, the two centers began trashing each other. McBride watched it for less than two minutes when he stopped the game, called the two centers to him and said, "Gentlemen, I want to tell you something and I want you to listen real close. The other referee and I did not drive one hundred miles to hear you guys call each other names.

"Now, be advised. The next guy who refers to ancestry, native country or anything else is gone from this game . . . that's a promise and I advise you not to try me. So, clean it up and let's play basketball."

Both centers played an excellent game and there was no more trashing. After the game ended, the Brazil center came to McBride and said, "You are the first referee to straighten out the trashing all year. We played basketball and I loved it. No more trashing from me."

On the way home, Oler said, "I learned a valuable lesson tonight. Take charge early."

McBride learned this when he was a rookie referee and was working a game between the professional New York Renaissance and a Richmond All-Star team. There was a definite charge directly in front of him, but he did not make the call. A few minutes later, there was another charge and this time McBride whistled the foul. James (Pappy) Gates, a great player with the Rens, walked over to McBride and said, "Son, if you get the first one, you never have to worry about the second one." It was advice the Richmond referee never forgot.

One thing McBride was well known for among referees was that he never made his partner look bad. He learned this lesson at an early age.

In his first year, McBride was working with veteran official Karl Dickerson in a game between two southern Indiana schools. In the second period, Dickerson, the out official, called a travel that apparently happened right in front of McBride.

"There absolutely was no travel and I was right on top of it," said the referee. "The guard spun around but kept his pivot foot solid. I could not believe Dickerson would make me look bad on such a call, but knew I would have the chance to get even."

Before the half ended, McBride saw a player lift his pivot foot only a few feet from the other referee and he called it from under the basket. Dickerson glared at him but said nothing until they got to the dressing room at halftime.

"Kid," said Dickerson, "we don't do that in this league."

"Karl," answered McBride, "you did it to me. You called a travel directly in front of me and the boy did not travel. If you do it again, I will blow you clear out of this gym."

A few days later, McBride saw one of the best officials in the state, Clab Robinson, and the Connersville referee grinned and said, "You shook Dickerson up. He told me about your remark the other night and said you really are a cocky character. I told him that indeed you were cocky, but not to bet you wouldn't do exactly what you said you would do."

In the days when a timer had to keep the clock going at

the bench, getting caught up in the game could result in problems. Martinsville was playing at Connersville and Charlie Heck, the Spartan athletic director, was the timer. The game was a scorcher and went into overtime.

The lead changed hands twice before Martinsville hit two quick baskets for a four point lead and Connersville called a time out. McBride, who was wearing a watch, went to the bench to see how much time was left. Heck told him ninety seconds. McBride glanced at the time on his watch and play resumed.

Connersville lost the ball out of bounds and Martinsville scored again. Down came the Spartans and hit to close it to four points. But they could not get any closer as Martinsville matched them basket for basket.

Suddenly McBride looked at his watch and realized they had been playing a full five minutes. He grabbed the ball, blew his whistle until the crowd quieted so he could be heard and yelled, "This game is over."

As he walked toward the dressing room, Connersville Coach Ken Gunning came running after him.

"Hey, Mac," he shouted, "what are you doing. You can't stop the game, that is the timer's call."

"Ken," answered the referee, "Charlie told me we had a minute and a half to go and we played five. What were we going to do, play until you got ahead?"

Just then, Heck came into the dressing room and said, "Ken, don't get on him. Mac, I apologize. I got caught up in the game and forgot to start the clock."

A referee must be on his toes every moment. When his concentration breaks down, there's only one other option in the call—the other referee.

The game was at Columbus when McBride found himself with a touchy problem. It could have resulted in disaster.

A Jeffersonville guard fired a long one from half court as the game came down to the final seconds, and was fouled on the play. McBride signaled the foul and quickly turned to see if the shot went through. The ball was dropping to the floor and he could not tell. He hurried over to Hilligoss and asked, "Did the shot go through, John?"

Sheepishly Hilligoss said, "I don't know, Mac. Jonas Markey [formerly of Richmond, then living in Columbus] hollered at me and I was looking at him."

The senior official hurried over to the Columbus radio announcer and asked, "Did that shot go in?"

"Why are you asking me?"

"Because neither one of us saw it and if I ask the Jeffersonville sports writer, he is going to say yes. And if I ask the Columbus sports writer, he is going to say no. But you already have told everyone on the air whether it hit or not. So did it go in or not?"

The announcer grinned and said, "That is pretty good logic. Yes, it went in." So, McBride turned to the bench and signaled two points.

"In all our years working together," said McBride, "that is the only time Hilligoss ever let me down."

8

McBride A Globetrotter!

Don McBride can boast to this day that he played for the world famous Harlem Globetrotters. And he is telling the truth.

The Globetrotters were to perform at Richmond, and McBride was asked to work the game with one of the greatest referees of all time, Pat Kennedy. Kennedy was the lone referee traveling with the Trotters and a second official was hired locally. McBride said the game had gone exceptionally well until midway through the fourth quarter. Let him tell it:

"Goose Tatum, the Globetrotter all-star, took a pass under the basket and then waved off the opposition. Suddenly two of their players picked me up and carried me to the basket. Tatum handed me the ball and said, 'Dunk it.' The big Trotters lifted me until I was even with the basket and to the roar of the crowd, I slammed it through."

For years, if anyone asked McBride whether he played professional basketball or not, he truthfully could say, "I most certainly did. I played with the Globetrotters."

Kennedy taught McBride to be firm in his calls and from that Globetrotter game forward, if he made a call, it was, "You pushed" . . . or . . . "you charged" . . . or . . . "you hacked" . . . or . . . "you traveled" . . . or . . . "you're holding." On a foul, McBride would go to the scorer's bench and yell, "It's a charge" . . . or . . . "it's a hold" . . . or . . . "it's a hack" . . . or . . . "it's a push." He never left anything in doubt.

Also, the referee believed in relaxing the players when the chance arose. For example, often, as a player stepped to the free throw line, especially in a close game, McBride would say, "Hey, kid, this one is for the girls. Relax and hit it."

McBride said the key to being a good official consists of several things.

"You must be in position to see the play . . . always keep moving . . . the word hustle is double for a referee . . . act like you are enjoying the game, the players and the fans . . . dress neatly and look like an official . . . be physically in shape . . . interpret the rules as the book says . . . take charge of the game early and work in cooperation with the other official.

"A referee can change the course of a game, if he is not doing his job properly. He must not blow his whistle because of who he is or what game he is working, but only for a violation. Restrict calls to things that happen, not what might happen. Don't anticipate. And if you call every touch on the floor, there will be no players left to finish the game."

An example of the rewards for using these keys came to McBride and Hilligoss after the former had retired and the latter had passed away.

McBride and some cronies went to New Castle to watch a tournament, and between afternoon and evening sessions, the four men went to Knightstown to eat. While seated at a table, they could hear six men at another table really letting the tournament referees have it.

"They couldn't keep up."

"Yeh, and they don't know the rules."

"That one ref kept calling fouls under the basket when he was at the center line." And on and on.

Finally, McBride turned to the other table and said, "You guys are getting on the refs pretty hard. I didn't think they were that bad."

"Mister," asked one of the men, "did you ever see McBride and Hilligoss referee?"

"A couple of times," answered McBride.

"Now there was a pair . . . super officials . . . put these guys to shame. Wish they were back."

McBride turned back to his companions and with a grin said, "So do I." The fan never knew he was talking to the Richmond official.

McBride may have been a master in talking his way out of most all of the situations on a basketball court, but he learned the hard way it doesn't work with the Internal Revenue Service (IRS).

"I forgot to turn in a W-2 form from a tournament at Indianapolis Tech and was called in for an audit. It only amounted to $75, so I told the IRS representative that we did not make any money from refereeing.

"We are allowed one meal, dry cleaning expenses, mileage and little else," said the referee.

"Why do you do it, then?" asked the tax man.

"I love the game," answered the referee. "There is a thrill out there that cannot be matched. It is the game, the players, the fans, yes, and even the coaches. It is a way of life and I always strive to do my best."

McBride was sure he had gotten through to the IRS man, for he seemed to be highly interested in what the referee had to say.

"It has been interesting to talk with you," said the man.

"Your penalty for not turning in your W-2 form will be . . . !"

Even after retirement, McBride had his fun on the floor. He was asked to work a benefit game at Lynn (Randolph Southern High School). He agreed on the basis he would work from center court and the school would have two more referees, one at each end of the floor.

Unbeknown to anyone, McBride put a track starting pistol in his pocket and the first time a player went flying by, he pulled it out and fired into the air, scaring the wits out of the dribbler. "Slow down. I can't keep up," yelled McBride, to the delight of the fans.

The Richmond referee said it is the off-hand remarks of

coaches and players that make basketball officiating worthwhile.

Attucks Coach Ray Crowe and Attucks great Bailey Robertson were headed for the dinner where Bailey would be inducted into the Basketball Hall of Fame when they saw McBride.

"Hey coach," said Bailey, "here is the referee who fouled me out of every game he worked."

"Not true Bailey, not true," said McBride.

"Bailey," said Crowe, "if every referee in the state had been as fair to us as McBride, we never would have had any gripes about the officiating."

Bailey, with a big grin, said, "Only kidding, Mac. You were the best."

There were times when a referee, trying to be nice, found out he had to back off and pay the consequences. Hilligoss was running for city council in Richmond. To promote his campaign, he had a truck load of miniature whistles made up with his name on the side. It made no difference to him where he was or whether the voters could vote for him or not, Hilligoss loved to pass out those whistles.

He and McBride were at Rushville for a game and a fan at the end of the gym yelled at Hilligoss, "Hey, I've heard about your miniature whistles. How about giving me one?"

"Sure," answered Hilligoss. So he went to the car and brought in a couple hundred and handed them to the fan. He passed the box around until they were gone.

The game started and on the first call, 202 whistles blew in unison. McBride stopped the game, turned to Hilligoss and said, "You passed them out, you go get them."

The red-faced official got the box and had all the fans return them and he was soundly booed as he did so. The cry of, "Indian giver, Hilligoss," echoed throughout the gym the rest of the evening.

When a referee knows a call must be made and that he will be highly criticized for it, he has no choice. It may well have been the hardest decision McBride ever had to make.

The call occurred in the Kentucky-Indiana All-Star game at Indianapolis in 1960. Angus Nicoson, Indiana Central coach, headed up the Indiana stars and was trailing by one point with seconds to go when one of his players leaped high to intercept a pass and then, apparently, drove for the basket and hit what would have been the winning goal.

However, as the player came down with the steal, he took two steps in his anxiety to break down the floor and McBride whistled traveling. Suddenly he realized his whistle had not been heard over the screaming of the crowd in Butler Fieldhouse and he went down the floor waving off the field goal.

"I honestly believe everything laying loose was tossed at me from the stands," said the referee, "but I could never have lived with myself if I had not made the right call."

The Richmond referee had a second sense when it came to recognizing a problem and working it out before it started. Two centers from small schools were in their first regional at Indianapolis, and McBride saw they were nervous as they came to go over instructions.

"Boy, there sure are a lot of people here," said one of the players.

"Yeh," chimed in the other center. "I hope I don't make a fool of myself on the jump."

"Hey, you guys," said McBride. "All you got to do is jump. I got to throw the ball up and did you ever see a ball go up making a figure eight?"

Both centers laughed, it broke the tension, and the tip went off without a hitch.

"Some coaches did not like the way I tried to keep the kids relaxed," said the referee, "but my philosophy was, if they didn't like it, they did not have to hire me back."

Several years after his whistle had been hung up for the last time, McBride was at Randolph Southern in Lynn, evaluating two young officials. At halftime there was a drawing and Barbara Hines talked McBride into buying a ticket. To this day he believes she palmed it, for it was drawn. The announcer made a production out of announcing that the former referee had won a basketball.

McBride walked over to the sideline, spotted a boy some ten years of age and said, "Son, do you like to play basketball?" "Yes, sir," answered the lad.

"Well, here is a ball you can play with from now on," and he tossed the ball to the boy.

A woman seated nearby, who was old enough to have seen the referee in his heyday, smiled and said, "McBride, you're not all bad after all!"

McBride was well known for his camaraderie with the players, but there were other officials with the same ability. "Tubby Trobaugh was one of these," said Joe Mullins. "He was not the best basketball official in the game, but after calling a foul, he would whistle between his teeth and say to the shooter, 'Come on buddy, come on buddy, let's get her going.' The kids really liked him and because of his style, he got little criticism from the coaches."

It was not unusual for referees to get in odd situations on the floor, but when it happened away from play, it added to the excitement. Here are two examples. In the early sixties, Bob Spay was working the Indianapolis regional with McBride and Hilligoss and was the alternate official on the championship game. It was between Crispus Attucks and Anderson, and was a close game throughout. In the waning moments, Attucks lost and the two floor officials dashed for the dressing room.

Spay, however, seated near the scorer's bench, had a lot farther to go, and as he reached the last aisle, a huge man jumped in front of him. The referee sidestepped and went past the fan, but then realized the man was chasing him.

"He was screaming, 'What do you mean cheating Attucks like that! You cost them the game,' plus a few more unspecified words. I must admit I was apprehensive for he was big enough to chew me up and spit me out. Just then," said Spay, "a policeman grabbed the guy and ushered him out. When I reached the dressing room, McBride asked, 'Where have you been?' I told him what happened and added, 'he didn't get to me, but it was close.'"

The senior official laughed and said, "Bob, you must be the worst official in the history of Indiana. That is the first time I have ever heard of anybody attacking the alternate."

Referees Jim Bozwell, Wendell Baker and John Thomas were headed for the regional finals at Terre Haute when they ran into slowed traffic east of Brazil on U.S. 40. Traffic had been heavy since they left Indianapolis and suddenly they realized they were going to run close on time. Let Thomas tell it:

"We did not have the radio on and were not aware there had been a bank robbery in Brazil. We found out later that three men were seen driving away in a dark colored car. I pulled over at the east edge of Brazil and told Wendell to drive while Jim and I got in the back seat to change into our referee clothes.

"We slipped off our shoes as we went through town, commenting on how many policemen there were, still dumb to what had happened. As we cleared the west end of Brazil, we got down to business and started stripping. We were down to the buff when Wendell said there was a flashing light back of us and he pulled over.

"Now, if you want a scare, have a state policeman walk up to your car with the flap open on his gun holster and his hand resting on the butt of the gun. He flashed his light into the back seat of the car as he passed and stopped cold. His light picked up the bare behinds of two men who were doing all possible to keep some dignity. The trooper stepped to the open front window of the car, laughed and said, 'Obviously, you guys haven't been robbing a bank dressed like that.'

"No," said Thomas, "but we sure need to get going if we are to get to Terre Haute for the regional final. We are referees."

Ever Wonder Where A Referee Worked?

Referees whose careers are described in this book came from many fields of endeavor.

DON MCBRIDE worked for a wholesale drug company, sold sporting goods and was Richmond park superindentent.

JOHN HILLIGOSS was a factory supervisor.

CY BIRGE sold sporting goods for a Jasper company. KARL BLY was a coach and teacher and football referee. SCOOP CAMPBELL worked for a Dunkirk manufacturing company. CHARLIE FOUTY headed a newspaper advertising department. ROSALIE (ROSIE) LEEDY is a high school counsellor. DICK and DANNY JACOBS worked in a Bloomington factory.

FRED MARLOW was a salesman for the Filter Queen Corporation. BILL MAY worked as an accountant. JOE MULLINS was a teacher.

CHARLIE NORTHAM sold automobiles and life insurance. HOMER OWENS, JR. was a farmer. C.N. PHILLIPS was a banker. HOWARD PLOUGH taught school.

FRANK SANDERS was a teacher and principal.

BOB SHOWALTER presently is an elementary principal. LOWELL SMITH is a farmer at Palmyra near Jeffersonville. DON SNEDEKER farms east of Connersville.

BOB SPAY worked for a manufacturing company in Kokomo. JOHN THOMAS is a banker.

GLEN WISLER was district manager for Production Credit Association.

Again the trooper laughed, "Commissioner Eskew is a good friend of mine and he's got to hear about this."

"Sure enough," Thomas added, "the trooper did call Eskew and the commissioner used this story at banquets on several occasions."

The unusual also happened on the court although in this case, the fan never knew how right he was. It was a 1969 Richmond sectional game and late in the third period, two players collided on a fast break and both fell to the floor grabbing their mouths. The two referees, Jim Frey and Darrel McFall, hurried to the two players and said something to them. Both boys opened their mouths wide and one referee checked out one mouth while the other referee checked out the mouth of the second player.

At the scorers bench, tournament official Dudley Johnson heard a Richmond fan remark, "Look at those two referees, now they think they are dentists." They were! Frey was a dentist from Fort Wayne and McFall was a dentist at Carmel.

Coaches were notorious for doing anything that would give their teams an advantage. Putting the opposing team out of direct line with the scoreboard was common practice. Having a backboard that jiggled was another. But Julius (Bud) Ritter at Madison, was the king of them all when it came to improper tricks.

Thomas tells this story:

"If Bud's team was playing one that loved to fast break, he would have the janitor put a net on his end of the floor that would not allow the ball to quickly drop through. This gave his players a chance to get up court.

"I was officiating the Jeffersonville-Madison game, and as we readied to start the second half, Red Devil Coach Bill Johnson came hurrying over.

"John," he said, "I was told that while we were in the dressing room the janitor changed the net on our end of the floor."

"Yeh," I answered, "I have heard the rumor that Bud does that."

Thomas walked over to the Madison coach and ask for a basketball. "What for?" asked Ritter. "I want to see how fast it goes through your net," answered the referee.

Ritter grinned and said, "Okay, you redheaded devil, do your thing."

"We got a pair of scissors and cut the lower strings of the new net, until the ball dropped through with ease."

Thomas officiated one of the biggest upsets Aurora ever had to face. In fact, there were some red faces when it was over, plus honors bestowed for a job well done.

"It was a case of Principal Gabbard and Coach Harry Ritter counting their chickens before they were hatched," said Thomas.

Aurora was picked to win the state. Their route through the sectional and regional seemed clear, not facing a team with power until the semistate.

"Jim Patterson had the sectional with me," said Thomas, "and upon arriving, we learned that Aurora had purchased new uniforms for its players, but had decided not to wear them until the regional. Jim made the statement to me that that could well be a kiss of death."

Ritter's team breezed through its first two games and on Saturday night was to meet Vevay for the championship. Vevay, under first-year Coach John Collier, had a mediocre year and most all basketball fans were hoping Aurora would not embarrass its opponent with a big score.

"Instead," said Thomas, "Vevay made a game of it from the opening tip and I quickly realized Collier had a well-coached team. It was one of the best games Jim or I had ever worked, with few fouls, lots of good action and two excellent teams. It ended with Vevay upsetting the potential state champions.

"Our dressing room was the stage area at one end of the gymnasium, and we hurried there to change clothes. We had stripped to our jockstraps when timekeeper Pat

O'Neil came around the curtain and asked if we would put towels around us and go with him. I must admit," Thomas said, "we thought something must be wrong and we were going to be roasted.

"Instead," he continued, "as we stepped around the curtain, we saw the gymnasium still jammed with people and both teams still on the floor. A man passed a microphone up to O'Neil and he said, 'Ladies and gentlemen, what have we got to say to these two guys who worked this basketball tournament?' We got a standing ovation, the greatest moment of my referee days."

That wasn't all.

"I looked at the floor," said Thomas, "and knew the Aurora players were in shock over losing in the sectional. But they, to a man, also were clapping their hands for us. It doesn't get any better than that."

The veterans often had to calm the rookies or basketball might well have lost some excellent referees. Karl Bly was working a B-team game in his first year as an official, and he made the Connersville players pull their arms in on free throws.

"They were extending their arms out over the foul lane and wiggling their hands to disrupt the shooter. I made them stop it and suddenly their coach Art Gross was at my side raving and ranting. I ordered him to the bench, but it did little good as he raved on and on. I was so new, I didn't know what to do. Gross made it miserable for me the rest of the game and when I entered the dressing room at the close, I slammed my whistle against the wall and said, 'I quit, that's it, I quit.'

"Griz Baker, a veteran referee and football coach at New Castle, told me to calm down and then he said, 'Karl, there is nothing wrong with your basics or your fundamentals. You know the rules. But when you blow that whistle, blow it as loud as you can, point as far as you can and everybody will think you know what you are doing, whether you do or not.'

"I followed that rule for nineteen years as a referee," said Bly, "and found it hard to call it quits."

Speaking of shooting free throws, Del Harris has a favorite story he tells at banquets. "In one of our games at Dale High School, a Catholic boy stepped to the line for a free throw and crossed himself. My guard, standing to the right of the shooter, did the same thing, only he was not Catholic.

"The boy at the line complained to the referee that my player was mocking him.

"'No Mr. Ref'," said my guard, "while crossing himself he said, 'I . . . hope . . . I . . . hit.' When I crossed myself I said, 'I . . . hope . . . you . . . miss.'"

Indianapolis Referee Frank Baird, who coached at Broad Ripple for several years, said he greatly enjoyed McBride and his antics for one special reason. "Don would stop and talk to the crowd, or spend time making a point with a coach and it would give me a chance to catch my breath."

The fans at Lafayette also enjoyed McBride's showing up as referee, especially when Marion football coach Mark Surface's father, who seldom missed a Jeff game, was there. He always sat in the front row, near the scorers bench, and he could imitate the referee's cocky walk to perfection. McBride would go strutting across the floor and the fan would strut down the sideline, much to the enjoyment of all, even the referee.

The Richmond official found it interesting the different methods used by different teams to get ready for a game. Scott Fisher, coach at Muncie Burris, may have had the most unique workout.

McBride was in Muncie on business and decided to stop and see Fisher. When he arrived at the Ball State fieldhouse, he saw a group of boys pitching horseshoes and Fisher standing off to one side. "What's this all about?" asked McBride, as he walked up to the coach.

"Mac," answered the coach, "if they can hit that little post, they surely can hit that bigger goal."

It must have worked, for in 1942, star player Skeeter Salyer helped take the Owls to the final game of the state tourney, where they lost to Washington High School, 24-18.

The Richmond official always has said there were players in many of the small schools who could have been Indiana All Stars if they had been on a major team. Lynn's Bill Maines was one of them.

"Bill had all the moves," said McBride, "and could have started on any team in the state. Bill was right handed," he continued, "but I was calling a game one night when he stole the ball at mid-court and went under the basket with two men on him. As he went up, he switched the ball from his right to his left hand and used the goal to keep his shot from being blocked. It was an impossible shot, at the speed he was going, but he hit it."

As McBride went down the floor, the opposing Coach Howard Rust yelled, "He traveled."

"Howard," answered McBride, "if he did, he did it so quickly I sure didn't see it. I've got the whistle and no travel."

Oddly enough, the other small school player McBride ranks in a class with Bill Maines is Bill's brother Joe, leader of the team that gave the small school at Lynn its lone sectional title in 1950.

"There were many others," said McBride, "Ted Kaufman at Brownsville, Lyle Kidd at Everton and, although a bigger school, the best eastern Indiana individual player I ever saw was John (Ossie) Logan from Richmond."

The true camaraderie between referees and coaches comes out when someone in either profession is hurting. McBride and Hilligoss went to New Castle for a game soon after the extremely well-liked player and coach, Ray Pavy, had been severely injured in an automobile accident. Horace Cook, the athletic director at New Castle, told

McBride they were starting a fund to help Pavy with the medical expenses.

"Horace," said the Richmond referee, "you take my check for tonight and put it in the fund, and you tell every referee who comes in here that I urge them to do the same." Hilligoss also signed his check over to the fund.

Later in the year, McBride talked again with the athletic director and found that is exactly what happened. Every referee who worked at New Castle turned his check over to the Pavy fund. "Ray is a super individual," said McBride, "and there were many in the basketball realm who were more than happy to help him in any way we could."

In earlier years, Cecil Tague coached at New Castle and was involved in the most unusual beginning of any game in Indiana basketball history. The game was at New Castle with Noblesville the opponent. Fred Marlow was the senior official.

"New Castle went through the warm-ups without problems," said Marlow, "but when they readied for the opening tip-off, Noblesville Coach Glen Harper came to me and said none of the numbers on the backs of the players jibed with the numbers the scorers bench had been given. Coach Tague tried to explain that in his excitement in having his star player back for this game after a suspension, he had given the scorer the away team numbers instead of home numbers.

"So I whistled one technical for each player with a wrong number in the starting line up," Marlow continued. "The game opened with Noblesville shooting five free throws and getting the ball out of bounds."

Let Tague tell the rest of the story:

"George Barber was the player who had returned to the lineup, one of the best in New Castle history. After the T's were called, the Noblesville player hit five straight, got the ball out of bounds and immediately scored again. With six seconds gone in the game, we were trailing, 7-0.

"I saw Barber smiling as he came down the floor and I told him it wasn't funny. We were down seven and if I lost this game on such a dumb error, I would get run out of town.

"There was only a minute to go in the quarter when I saw the officials whistle a time-out and point at my bench. I yelled, I didn't call a time-out, who did? They told me Barber had.

"Why in the world did you do that?" I yelled at him in the huddle. "He grinned and said, 'I just wanted to see if you were feeling better.' We were leading, 22-8."

Athletic directors were not beyond trying to jab a referee and Pop Davidson at Farmland carried a sharp needle. Davidson also was the coach and before the game started, told McBride, "I don't have a very good team this year and we'll lose this one tonight by a wide margin. Since it won't be a close game, that means you won't have to work very hard. Do you suppose you could take less pay for the game?"

McBride quickly started to defend himself by saying, "Never," when he saw Davidson's shy grin and knew he was being put on.

"It was guys like Pop who made the job of refereeing so much fun," said McBride. "I remember how Cloyce Quakenbush at Fountain City would have his players change numbers at halftime, just to goof us up. Or how some coaches became clones of other coaches, such as John Mutchner, who became an exact pattern of Bob Warner.

"Some," he continued, "wanted more than they were entitled to. You had to learn the inside of a coach in order to do the job right for him. This took time, but it also took instinct."

However, it did not always work. And when a coach did pull something unexpected that did not violate the rules, McBride had to laugh and accept the position of being conned.

McBride had been warned that Don (Wimpy) Worthman, coach at Decatur, could become a wild man during a game, pacing the sidelines and generally causing all kinds of chaos.

Before the first game of the Fort Wayne regional got underway, McBride went to the coach and said, "I've heard about your antics, so stay on the bench. I don't want to nail you here in the tournament, but I will if you don't stay on that bench."

"No need to worry," answered Worthman. "I'll not get off the bench, I promise."

Through the first quarter, Worthman lived up to his word. He never left the bench and his team was playing good ball.

But as the second quarter got underway, Decatur players had three consecutive turnovers, and as a ball went out of bounds to the opposing team, the second referee, Stan Dubis yelled at McBride, "Look at Wimpy!"

The Richmond referee said he couldn't believe his eyes, but then he knew he had been had. All of the Decatur reserve players were sitting on the floor and their coach was running up and down on top of the bench, waving his arms and screaming at the top of his lungs.

"What are you going to do now?" asked Dubis.

"Nothing," laughed McBride, "he outfoxed me."

One of the most controversial calls a referee can make is getting someone for an illegal block, or as the coaches say, a pick. Franklin was playing at Lawrenceburg and in the second quarter, McBride had an out-of-bounds directly in front of the Lawrenceburg bench.

"Hey, Mac," yelled Coach Bateman, "watch their picks. They are moving. It's a foul."

McBride glanced at him, laughed and said, "Bud, I wish I had a nickel for every time I've called an illegal pick on your team. You are a master at using them. So be quiet."

Bateman hollered back, "You can't blame me for trying."

It seems impossible, but there are certain coaches referees can't seem to call a good game for, and it is a mystery why this happens.

"Al Brown was coach at Knightstown," said McBride, "and Hilligoss and I had an early-season game. John worked for the Belden Corporation in Richmond and he brought his boss from Chicago to watch us referee. We called a horrible game.

"Brown came to the dressing room after it was over and I said, 'Al, don't pay us, we did a terrible job. I promise when we come back next year, we will work a good one for you.'"

It was a promise McBride should not have made. For when he and Hilligoss returned to Knightstown the following year, "We again called a lousy game," said McBride. "How do we know when we do a poor job?" he added. "It is a super sense referees have, similar to a speaker who knows whether his talk is good or not."

"We never worked for Al after that," said the Richmond official, "and not at his request, we simply knew we could not give him a good game for some unknown reason."

After a referee reached the point of being in demand, he refused to be intimidated by the coaches, often canceling a contract if he thought the coach was using wrong tactics. Gary Roosevelt was at Lafayette Jeff and during the first half, Coach Bo Ballard had them playing good, clean basketball. By halftime, McBride and Hilligoss had called only three fouls on the visitors.

On the other hand, Jeff Coach Marion Crawley's players were picking and screening, causing excessive fouls. By halftime, Jeff had eleven called its way.

While the two referees were resting in the dressing room, in came the Jeff official scorer. He said:

"Mr. McBride, Mr. Crawley said that eleven on us and only three on them is not very even."

"You go back and tell Mr. Crawley that there is nothing in my contract that says the fouls are supposed to be even. You tell him that if they end up twenty-two and six, and that is the way it happened, then that is the way it is going to be." Oddly enough, Jeff won the game on two free throws in the closing seconds, one of only eight fouls called against Gary Roosevelt in the game.

In the dressing room, after the game, McBride said the more he thought about the coach sending his scorer to try and influence him, the madder it made him. As he and Hilligoss were leaving, Crawley glanced their way and said, "Good game, fellas."

McBride answered, "Marion, it wasn't a good game. I did not appreciate your antics at halftime. So, tear up my contract for next year, I won't be back."

"You also can tear up mine," added Hilligoss.

"We never worked for Marion again, except when his team was playing at an away gymnasium," said McBride. "Yet, I never considered him an enemy and, in fact, went with former Commissioner Phil Eskew to his funeral."

On the opposite side, when a coach came to the dressing room after a game and congratulated the referees for a good job, especially when that coach lost, it made the officials feel good and developed better relationships between both parties.

Dominick Polizotto and McBride worked the afternoon 1952 New Albany-Muncie Central state tourney game and it was a scrap. After it ended, New Albany Coach Gordon Rainey came to the dressing room and said, "Gentlemen, I must admit, when I heard we had two northern officials working this game, I was concerned. But you two worked the best game I have ever had worked for me." The oddity here is, that game was vital to both teams and New Albany lost by one point, 68-67.

The Richmond referee said Don Odle, now retired as coach of Taylor University, was an excellent coach and gentleman, even in his high school coaching days at Aurora. "If Don disagreed with a call," said McBride, "he would quietly say to me as I went by the bench, 'Wasn't that last one a little questionable?'

"Aurora had, a better-than-average team, with one of the small schools best forwards," McBride continued. "This

High School Basketball Popularity Waning

In a survey of Golden Age referees, an overwhelming majority see the popularity of Indiana high school basketball waning.

Karl Bly, a retired referee, teacher and coach, correctly assessed the problem. "Our high schools are struggling financially. As athletic departments have expanded, revenue from attendance at basketball games has gone down. During the Golden Age, a losing team at a small school still filled the gymnasium. Today a losing team plays before an empty fieldhouse."

What are the reasons for this decline in attendance? "Television coverage of college basketball ranks as the prime factor," says retired Big Ten official Bob Showalter, an elementary principal. "People will not show up at local games if there is a prime college game on TV."

"Have you noticed," added Don McBride, "if Indiana or Purdue has a televised game, none of the bigger state colleges, such as Butler, Ball State, Evansville, Indiana State or Notre Dame, schedule a game that night. Television sets the schedule and financial needs necessitate going along with it."

"It is not only basketball," said former referee and retired teacher Frank Sanders. "You do not schedule any school event on a night when IU or Purdue is playing if you want a good attendance. People simply will not show up."

"There are thousands of automobiles with either Indiana or Purdue license plates who would have a hard time finding the campuses," asserts Terre Haute resident Charlie Fouty, also a retired Big Ten referee. "People feel they are part of the university simply because they watch every game that is on TV."

Homer Owens Jr., a retired referee but also a former member of the Union School Board, summed it up this way:

"Because of television, college ball continues to gain in popularity and high schools are taking the brunt of this trend. Indiana remains the No. 1 state in the nation for high school basketball but no longer does a school revolve around its team as it did before the days of school consolidation."

was in the days of four fouls and out. With only four minutes gone in the third quarter, he picked up his third foul.

"At the next time-out, I was some ten feet from Odle
when he glanced at me and said, 'Don, the boy with three
is most of my ball club.'

"Don," answered McBride, "I haven't committed one
foul." Odle grinned and said, "I get your point."

The Golden Age has long since passed. Today referees
are instructed not to socialize with the players or coaches
on the floor. Everything must go by the book, and showboating is not simply frowned upon, it is outlawed.

The pure basketball fan will tell you it has taken the
fun out of the game. No longer do the rafters ring with, "Its
a charge." No longer do the fans circle the gymnasium floor,
becoming part of the action. In fact, in most Indiana high
schools today, new gymnasiums are half filled night after
night. Those who are there mill around, many seeing less
than half of the game. The excitement seldom reaches a
frenzied pitch as it did during the Golden Age.

Yet, with all the changes, Indiana still remains the No.
1 basketball capital of the world. In the minds and hearts
of the true basketball fan, the movie *Hoosiers* brought back
a revival of the Golden Age. Bobby Plump still is recog-
nized and remembered for his one jump shot. Oscar and
Larry and Rick and George are names that need no last
name in Indiana lore.

Maybe Plump wrapped it up best when he said, "I am
honored that people still remember me after forty years.
But I am just one guy who was lucky enough to hit a shot
that would be remembered. I am concerned over the direction high school basketball is taking but as long as lights
still shine in an Indiana gymnasium, it will be our No. 1
sport."

And you, Bob and Oscar and Marion and Larry and
Rick and George, will always remain a vital part of the
Golden Age of Hoosier High School basketball.

> Former Big Ten Referee Bob Showalter: "The step from high school officiating to college is much bigger that from college to the pros. It take talent to reach the college level, but it also takes a lot of luck to stay there. I am pleased to say I had enough of both to spend seventeen years working in the Big Ten."

Preface: Overtime

A book on Indiana referees would not be complete without stories on those officials who worked college schedules. Because of the number, again those in the flow of this book worked with Don McBride either in high school or college.

Charlie Fouty, Bob Showalter and Cy Birge worked the Big Ten. Fouty became a close friend of IU Coach Bob Knight. Showalter had nothing but praise for Coach Gene Keady at Purdue. Birge considers John Wooden at UCLA the greatest coach he had the honor of working for. Each referee had a style of his own

Fouty was flamboyant. He took charge of a game from the opening tip and even Coach Knight listened when he spoke. In fact, his approach to refereeing may well be the reason he and Knight became friends. The ever present cigar in the corner of his mouth became a trademark, and on one occasion, the no smoking sign in the referee dressing room at IU was removed when Fouty was to work an important game.

Showalter was Mr. Consistency. It took him a while to be accepted and his two oldest children took the brunt of this in school, causing the referee to wonder whether he should give it up. But he did not retreat and became one of the premier officials of the Big Ten. He shook the Big Ten world of officiating when he became the first referee to wear glasses during a game.

Cy Birge worked the Big Ten for eleven years and had the UCLA game at Illinois when Lew Alcindor set a new scoring record. Birge was a referee who got the job done without extra effort and was well liked around the conference.

Don McBride, John Thomas, Glen Wisler, and Lowell Smith worked both high school and college. And there were many others who picked up a college game on an off night from high school or refereed a tournament to earn some extra money. As Fouty said, "College refereeing was far more serious than high school and yet, it had its moments."

In these two chapters we will bring you a few of those moments, reliving them through the eyes of those men who experienced the good and the bad at the college level.

It is their continuing story of the Golden Age.

From *Basketball Rules 1949–1950*, National Federation Edition.

9

A Few Referees Enjoyed
Both Levels

For some referees, high school "was it." Others preferred college games. Few really enjoyed both.

Don McBride and Cy Birge chose high school and both gave the same reason for enjoying the lower level competition.

"The players were there strictly for the love of the game," said the two officials, "and not because they were good enough to become famous in some big university program."

But for others, like Charlie Fouty and Bob Showalter, college was the real action and they loved it.

Still, as often happened when McBride had any game, his actions on the court make a story. In the early sixties, Western Michigan was playing at Manchester College in North Manchester, Indiana, and the visiting team had a Little All-American center. He knew he was good and did a lot of showboating during warmups.

In the second quarter the center camped inside the lane, violating the three second rule, and McBride whistled out of bounds to Manchester.

The center, holding the ball, glared at the referee and then slammed the ball at him as hard as he could. McBride said that had he tried to stop it, he would have broken his hand. The ball disappeared in the crowd.

"Son," said the referee, "you have ten seconds to get that ball and hand it to me.

Still glaring the center demanded, "Do you know who I am?"

"No," answered McBride, "but I'll tell you who I am. I'm the guy who is going to throw you out of this ball game if you do not get that ball back here in ten seconds, and you have already wasted five of them on an introduction."

The center still glared for a moment, then turned toward the crowd and a fan tossed him the ball. He walked over to the referee, handed him the ball and asked, "Is this the way you want it?"

"Son," McBride answered, "it isn't whether I want it this way or not, this is the way it's gotta be."

Play resumed and the Western Michigan center was on his best behavior the rest of the game.

There have been few better college referees than Charlie Fouty, a take-charge, no-nonsense guy. He started on the hardwoods in 1948 and went exclusively to college games in the fall of 1965. Fouty had the final game of the state high school tourney in 1965, the year Billy Keller and his Indianapolis Washington teammates defeated Fort Wayne North for the title.

Showalter began his high school career in 1954. He refereed the final state tournament game in 1970 when East Chicago Roosevelt pounded Carmel, 76-62. He credits Bob King, a friend since he was at Shortridge High School as an assistant to Coach Cleon Reynolds, for getting him in the Big Ten.

"Bob was at Purdue University by this time," said Showalter, "and he asked if I had ever thought of refereeing in the Big Ten? My first thought was, a country boy like me in the fast lane of major college basketball? No way.

"A few days later an application arrived in the mail, but I left it on my desk from May until September," said the referee. "A friend, Bill Hittle, saw it, said it would not cost me a thing to return it and urged me to do so.

"The next thing I knew I was in Chicago being interviewed and worked three games that first year." An odd thing happened before the season got underway.

"The annual Big Ten Officials Golf Tournament was held at Ann Arbor," said Showalter, "and I won. I hadn't worked a game in the conference to that date, but suddenly, here I was getting ready to accept a golf bag from Michigan Coach Johnny Orr. I must admit, I was feeling real good.

"Orr stepped to the microphone and said, 'The winner of this year's golf tournament is Bob Showalter from New Castle, Indiana, whoever the hell he is!' We became friends in later years and laughed about the incident, but it rather shook me that day."

As a college official, Fouty worked the Missouri Valley Conference and later, the Big Ten. He was well known for being in complete control of the game and for calling the least number of technical fouls of any Big Ten official.

"Where there is a rule violation," said Fouty, "then a technical must be called. But I have never seen a technical called that made a bad situation better."

"I have found out over the years," he continued, "that in most every situation, if you do not embarrass a coach the game will be much smoother. I go to a coach and say, 'Coach, I heard you. Let's play basketball.' And in most cases, he understood."

Fouty and Indiana Coach Bob Knight are friends, but it was not always that way.

Knight, then coach at Army, had his team playing in the 1970 Gator Bowl Classic against Florida State. Fouty and John McPherson, an excellent Southeastern Conference (SEC) official from Nashville, Tennessee, had the game.

In the dressing room prior to the tip off, SEC supervisor Cliff Harper asked, "Have either of you guys had this Army coach before?"

"We both shook our heads," said Fouty.

"Well," he continued, "I don't know what to tell you, but a couple weeks ago he kicked a water cooler over at Madison Square Garden and it took twenty minutes to clean up the glass and water."

John looked at Fouty and said, "Charlie, we have to

run into a horse's behind like that after we have driven a thousand miles to referee this game."

Let Fouty tell the story:

"Florida State had Dave Cowens at center and they were undefeated, an outstanding team. The game started and State soon was fourteen points ahead of Army.

"I had noticed the Army center was slow getting out of the three second lane, but I hated this call so I let it slide by. Finally, he stood in there for at least eight seconds and I blew the violation. My philosophy had always been, maybe one in one hundred referees can consistently count to three. My philosophy also is to call them at both ends of the floor exactly the same.

"I took the ball to give it to Florida State when I saw Knight pick up his metal chair and it collapsed to the hardwood with a loud bang. I laid the ball on the floor, walked over to him and asked, 'Coach, is there a problem?' He said, 'There sure as hell is. That is the worse call I have ever seen in basketball.' "

Fouty looked at him and said, "Coach, I wish you hadn't said that, for this game is not over and I can make them a whole lot worse than that."

The referee said Knight glared at him and said, "You're a smart SOB, aren't you?"

"No," said Fouty, "I am not trying to be. Coach, my buddy and I did not know a call like that would upset you so much, so I will tell you what . . . you call your kids over and tell them they can stay in the lane all evening and we will never make that call again tonight. But then I am going to go down and tell the Florida State coach that he can put his big redhead in the lane and leave him all night. We will forget about calling the three second violation."

Fouty said there was a good ten second pause, then Knight said, "Why don't we play basketball." The referee grinned and said, "That's a good idea."

On the next night, Fouty and McPherson had the championship game and after it was over, decided to go to a smorgasbord set up by the tournament committee for officials and coaches. They were seated near the back of the room when in walked Knight. He spotted them immediately, walked to where they sat, picked up a chair, turned it around and sat down astraddle the seat. "What's your name?" he asked Fouty. "Charlie Fouty." "Where you from?" "Terre Haute, Indiana."

Knight stared at the referee for a full thirty seconds, got to his feet, turned the chair around and walked off.

McPherson said, "Boy, he is going to write you up." But he didn't.

Two years later, Knight had left Army to accept the Indiana University coaching position and Fouty had been accepted as a Big Ten official. The annual Big Ten meeting to discuss rules changes and other aspects of the coming season was held at the University of Michigan. Fouty was sitting with several other referees chewing the fat when in walked Knight and Ohio State Coach Fred Taylor.

As they approached the group of referees, Knight pointed at Fouty and said, "Fred, there is the SOB I was telling you about." Taylor started laughing as Fouty got to his feet and said, "Coach, it's awful good to see you again."

"We shook hands," said the Terre Haute referee, "and I know people will not believe this, but I never had another problem with Bob Knight all the years I refereed."

Showalter said it took him five years to feel accepted. But once he earned the status of a veteran his stature grew with each game. "In my third year, I became discouraged," said Showalter. "I lived in New Castle. I was an elementary school principal in New Castle. We had first Kent Benson and later Steve Alford at IU from New Castle. If IU lost and I had the game, I might as well have had the plague. No one wanted to talk to me. If IU won, then the phone would ring off the hook, everyone wanting a piece of the action.

"Benson, a true gentleman, was on the cover of *Sports Illustrated* and a few nights later, I had the IU-Ohio State game when the Buckeyes upset the Hoosiers. Knight was furious with me, absolutely furious. He ranted and raved during the game. He ranted and raved on television. He ranted and raved on radio. He ranted and raved to reporters and then he called me at home and ranted and raved some more.

"Still considering myself a rookie, I listened to all he had to say and did not try to defend myself. I simply let him steam it all out. Later, I probably would have hung up on him, but in a way, I am glad I did not. When he was done screaming at me, he said, 'I'll see you at Bloomington Saturday,' and hung up. I had the Purdue at IU game that night.

"I could not help but wonder how I would be greeted by Knight at IU, or whether I would be shunned totally. There was nothing. It was over. We had an excellent game. I had had my baptism of fire.

"But," he continued, "there is a personal downside to this story. My two oldest children, one in junior high and the other in high school, were defending me over the OSU-IU incident. It ended in my son being beaten up and my daughter given a hard time for standing up for their father.

"My wife and I sat down with them and explained how at times fans can be misguided. I said they should not hold a grudge over what happened and that I was sure Coach Knight would not be pleased if he knew of the incident, for he is extremely protective of his children. But I must admit, it was a bitter pill to swallow."

Charlie Fouty came to this conclusion concerning the fiery coach of the Indiana Hoosiers.

"All Bob Knight ever wanted," said the referee, "was an official who would not lie to him and consistently referee the game. He is not one for excuses. And my advice is: don't make something up on a call that is not there."

Benson, Indiana's great center of the mid seventies, was a gentle giant, according to Fouty. But he was involved in a play that Knight, to this day, kids the referee for calling.

It was the 1974 Indiana-Michigan game, played on a neutral floor at the University of Illinois, where a playoff was held to settle the Big Ten title, something never done again after that year.

Fouty was working with Art White and Richie Weiler, both from Chicago, and early in the game the Terre Haute referee got Benson for goaltending. As he went down the floor, Knight yelled to the referee, "Dammit Fouty, that wasn't goaltending."

Fouty stopped the game, walked over to the bench and said, "Coach, how did it go in the scorebook?"

Knight never said another word about it during the game. Films of the call were not conclusive as to whether Fouty was right or Knight was right, but each time he got a chance to rub it in, the IU coach would let the referee know he needed to learn the violation of goaltending.

Showalter, as has been said, believes a referee needs both talent and luck to become a Big Ten official who is accepted.

"Ohio State was at Indiana and the Big Ten championship was on the line. Both teams were excellent with Herb Williams and Kelvin Ransey leading OSU, while this was the Mike Woodson era at IU," said Showalter.

"The lead constantly changed hands throughout the game and there was little doubt this might well go into overtime, or at least be decided by a last-second shot. Gary Muncy from Fort Wayne and Don Edwards from Grand Rapids, Michigan, were working it with me and we were ready for anything . . . we thought.

"It did go into overtime and with seconds to play, Williams fouled out and Muncy made the call. As he went by me he asked, 'do you have the shooter?' I said no, but I was sure Edwards would have him. When he said no, I remember thinking, oh my God . . . Big Ten championship . . . TV audience . . . and three clowns who, in the crucial part of the game, are going to come up wrong.

"We had a little time as OSU Coach Eldon Miller called time out," Showalter continued, "so we got together to discuss our problem . . . but with no satisfactory result. Muncy said we might get lucky and the right shooter walk to the line.

"The horn sounded and the teams came onto the floor. Woodson, IU's superstar, walked to the line and Muncy said, 'Woodson, I guarantee, you are not shooting these free throws.'

"Muncy knew it wasn't Woodson and he had a sense it might be Butch Carter," said Showalter, "IU's poorest free throw shooter. Muncy put him at the line.

"I waited for one of the two coaches to come unglued if we had the wrong shooter," the referee continued, "but nothing happened. We had the right shooter. Carter canned both free throws and IU had a one-point lead. I gave a sigh of relief, only to find myself within a second of really blowing it.

"OSU tossed in the ball and Ransey got in the open for a desperation shot. There was a red light on the scoreboard that came on automatically when time had run out and as I looked toward it, the light came on and the board showed three zeros. I saw the ball was not clear of Ransey's hand so I waved off the shot. At that point, with the ball clearly in the air, the horn sounded.

"If that ball goes in, I am dead," he continued. "I had waved it no shot and was headed for the dressing room and everyone in the fieldhouse heard the horn blow after my arms went into the air. But Ransey saved my life . . . he missed the shot. That night, luck, not talent, rode with me."

Using common sense can often stop a problem before it begins. Showalter ran into this with Purdue's Gene Keady. Purdue was at Ohio State and Showalter was standing by the scorers bench when Coach Keady came hurrying over. "Bob . . . Bob . . . that basket down there is crooked," he yelled, pointing to the opposite end of the floor.

"Oh," answered the referee.

"Yeh, look," said the Purdue coach, "you can see one side is lower than the other. It's gotta be changed."

"Gene," said Showalter, "I've been watching OSU warm up on it and they seem to be missing most of their shots. Anyhow, you are shooting at the good basket the first half."

"Oh, my," he answered, "I never thought of that. I would have time at the half to get it changed if it is wrong. Then we could shoot at two good baskets." The Purdue coach turned and hurried back to the bench and by halftime, had completely forgotten about the 'unlevel' basket.

"Gene Keady is an excellent coach," said Showalter, "and he does not hesitate to let you know if he disagrees on a call. But that bulldog look you see on television is strictly his game face. Away from the gymnasium he is a different person.

"In fact," Showalter added, "I probably had fewer problems with Keady than any other coach in the conference."

A referee can handle the gripes and growls of a coach, but there is one unwritten law. Never voice a doubt about the integrity of an official, nor say one word about his nationality or color.

Indiana was playing at Notre Dame in an early season game, and the Hoosiers were putting it on the Irish. As Fouty came down the floor, Notre Dame Coach Digger Phelps shouted, "Fouty, you sleeping with Knight?"

The referee immediately stopped the game, turned to Phelps and said, "Coach, I am going to tell you something right now. Don't you say another word to me tonight . . . nothing! Now, after tonight, you will not have to worry about it, for I will never work another Notre Dame ballgame. But . . . don't you say one more word to me tonight."

The referee called the Big Ten commissioner, who booked the Irish games, and told him to take his name off the Notre Dame schedule in the future for he refused to work there again. It never changed.

Fouty learned a valuable lesson from Jack Fette of Kansas City, one of the top referees of the Missouri Valley Conference.

"The game was in the old airplane hangar Bradley University at Peoria, Illinois, used for a gymnasium," said Fouty. "I had never met Fette before, but knew his reputation for taking control of a game early.

"The game was in mid-December and a non-conference outing with a Division II team from Minnesota. Fette walked to the center of the court, tossed the ball up to start the game and it went at an angle and not as high as it should have gone.

"Chuck Osborne was the Bradley coach and he yelled, 'Dammit Jack, throw it up higher and keep it straight.'

"A few minutes later, we had a tie-up on the Bradley end of the floor and again Fette did not throw the ball as high as Osborne wanted, so again he blasted the senior official. We made it to the half, but Osborne was on Fette constantly.

"In the dressing room Fette said, 'Kid, did you hear that so and so yelling at me? I'm going to teach him a lesson. No matter what I do to start the second half, don't blow your whistle.' Since this was my first Missouri Valley game, I wasn't about to interfere, so I simply said, 'yes sir.'

"On the floor, Fette lined the two teams up for the jump, bounced the ball a couple times and said, 'Here we go.' Then he proceeded to toss the ball high enough in the air that it banged off the bottom of the center scoreboard and fell to the floor.

"As a Bradley player took the ball on the bounce, Fette turned to Osborne and yelled, 'Coach, was that high enough for you?'

"After the game," continued Fouty, "we entered the dressing room and Fette said, 'Kid, there will be a knock on the door in a few minutes. You let me answer it.' Sure enough, within five minutes there was a knock and as Fette opened the door, there stood Osborne. He said, 'Okay if I come in a minute?'

"Fette swung the door open and said, 'Certainly coach. It's always a pleasure to have a man of your stature in our room. Come on in.' The coach closed the door, turned to Fette, put his hand on his shoulder and said, 'Buddy, you made a believer out of me tonight. You'll never hear another thing from me.'

"It also was a valuable lesson for me," said the Terre Haute official.

Rules are made to be followed. But there are times when a referee must bend those rules to make a point and Fouty saw this in an Ohio Valley Conference game with senior official Ralph Stout.

Stout was the mayor of Mountain City, Tennessee, and one of the best conference referees. The game was between Morehead State and Middle Tennessee and was being played in the new arena at Murfreesboro. The Morehead State coach had tangled with Stout before and there was no love lost between them.

"Stout tossed the ball up for the tip," Fouty continued, "and before it hardly hit a player's hand, the State coach was up screaming at the referee. It continued for eight solid minutes, never letting up for an instant, until we had a timeout.

"I walked over to Stout and said, 'Hey mayor, is someone yelling at you?' "

"You know damn well there is," he bellowed.

"How long are you going to put up with it?" Fouty asked.

"Watch," answered the senior official.

"The ball went in play," said Fouty, "and within five seconds I heard the whistle blow and Stout was heading for the State bench. I hurried over for I did not want to miss this.

"Stout stopped in front of the bench, crossed his arms and the State coach was letting him have it full force. He finally paused and Stout said, 'Coach, are you done eating me out? If you are, I'll tell you what we are going to do. We are going to play a little guessing game. I'm going to let you guess what line we are going to shoot from and who is going to shoot.'

"With this, Stout turned, signaled a technical, and walked to the Middle Tennessee bench and said to the coach, 'Give me a shooter.' Together, Stout and the player walked to the other end of the floor for the one technical shot. Stout handed him the ball and the boy missed the free throw. He turned to take the ball out of bounds and Stout said, 'Hey son, come back here. Shoot it again.' Again he missed the shot and again he turned away. 'Kid,' Stout said, 'try it one more time.' The shooter asked the referee how many times they were going to do this? Stout answered, 'Until you hit your shot . . . that's how long.' On this one the shooter canned it and Middle Tennessee got the ball out of bounds. The State coach never said a word.

"In the dressing room after the game," said Fouty, "Art Guepe, the Ohio Valley Conference commissioner, came walking in and said, 'Ralph, explain to me what went on out there.' 'Oh,' said Stout, 'the kid needed some free throw practice.' "

Fouty had an odd one happen when he worked at Morehead State in a game with Eastern Kentucky. "I actually had the president of State come on the floor and demand I call a technical foul on the opposing team for something a fan did to him in the stands. I could not laugh, for he was furious, but it was a foolish request, made in the heat of the moment.

"I finally got him calmed down and explained I could not let a college player shoot a free throw for something an adult did in the stands. I am not sure he ever understood my position."

Fouty was assigned to five NCAA finals and fourteen regionals. He considers the 1968 UCLA team with Lew Alcindor and the 1974-75-76 teams of Indiana University the best he has refereed. He had the game when IU star Scotty May broke his hand, ending the chances for Knight to have a national championship that year.

He did run into a problem, that turned out not to be a problem, prior to the 1968 tournament game between No. 1 and No. 2, UCLA and Houston.

In a meeting prior to the game, Fouty started to worry. He had been a player at Indiana State when John Wooden was the coach and now he had Wooden's team in the finals. So, when the tournament chairman, Pete Newell, readied to start the meeting, Fouty spoke up:

"Dr. Newell, before you get started, I want everyone in this room to know I played for Coach Wooden at Indiana State."

"Is that a concern of yours?" asked Newell. "Does that bother you?"

"No sir," said the referee, "not in the least."

Newell said, "You will work the Houston-UCLA game." The Terre Haute referee did so without any problems.

The infamous chair-throwing incident in the game between Indiana and Purdue had a side to it sports writers ignored. Fouty, a friend of the IU coach, was seated by the Hoosiers' bench and said the frustration that was perpetrated by the inaction of the referees is vital in understanding what Knight did. Fouty admits Knight was wrong in his actions.

"There was a loose ball in the backcourt and players on both teams kept fumbling it away," said Fouty. "Guys were all over the floor, jumping on top of each other, a really dangerous situation. The play ended in front of Knight. Films show that for nine seconds, an eternity in a situation like this, the referees did nothing. They could have called traveling. They could have called a jump ball. They could have called a foul. But they called nothing. They simply were not in control of the game.

"Finally, and to show you how off base they were, one referee signaled a jump ball and the other ref came running across the floor signaling a foul on IU's Marty Simmons for hitting Purdue guard Mark Atkinson's hand. Coach Knight came off the bench with his hands in the air, signaling a jump ball, but the referees ignored him.

"Purdue got the ball out of bounds but immediately the whistle blew and IU's Daryl Thomas was called for a foul on the toss-in. Knight jumped up to protest, to no avail, and as he was sitting down, made one last remark that caused the referee to turn toward the scorers bench and signal a technical. This time Coach was purple with rage. A nine-second delay in a call where someone could have been hurt, two different calls when one finally was made, a foul that films show never happened and the technical, simply proved to be more than even he could take.

"I do not know whether Knight threw the chair in anger or frustration, but I do know that after he was ejected and was walking across the floor, he stopped and turned, like he was heading back toward the referees. I was ready to stop him, even if he never spoke to me again. But he turned back and went to the dressing room and I went with him.

"As I said, Coach was wrong. But so were the officials wrong for precipitating what happened." The Terre Haute official had one last story on Knight, a side few people know about.

"On a Sunday morning, IU great Landon Turner was in a wreck going to Kings Island at Cincinnati. I was at a friend's house in Terre Haute when my wife called and said Knight was in Montana and was trying to reach me. In moments the phone rang and the IU coach asked, 'How bad is it?' I told him it didn't look very good. He told me he wanted me to do two things. One, pick him up at the Indianapolis airport and two, get hold of former Governor Otis Bowen and have him meet both of us at Methodist Hospital.

"Since I knew Bowen was on his way from Indianapolis to his home in Bremen, I called the State Police and they tracked him down. He quickly agreed to meet us at the hospital and I headed to the airport to pick up Knight.

"At the hospital, Knight and Bowen spent three hours with Turner's parents. I then took Knight to Bloomington and spent the night there. The next morning he was on the phone with Frank McKinney of American Fletcher bank. He told McKinney, 'Frank, we are setting up this trust fund for Landon and I want your trust department to handle it and dammit, Frank, there will not be any fees . . . you are going to handle it for nothing, Frank.'

"I never have seen a guy operate in twelve hours like Knight did with that trust fund. By the time it was over the fund was big enough to keep Turner for life. The three trustees of the fund were Knight, Bowen and then senator Birch Bayh.

"Do you see what I would have missed had I not made that decision several years ago to leave high school refereeing and enter the college ranks? It was a rewarding fifteen years."

When Fouty decided to hang it up, the decision came quickly and one day later, it was all over.

"I was headed home from the University of Illinois after working the last game of the 1979-80 Big Ten season," said the referee, "and there was a coating of ice on U.S. 36 that made driving hazardous. I was alone in the car, tired, fretting over the slick roads, when suddenly I said out loud, 'Fouty, what in the hell are you doing this for? You have been doing this for thirty years, never had an accident, never been hurt and you have worked everything there is to work. It is time to quit.'

"I finally made it home late on Saturday and on Sunday, called the Big Ten referee supervisor and said, 'I quit.' I have never regretted my decision." As with Fouty, Cy Birge and Bob Showalter agreed it was a lot easier ending a Big Ten refereeing career than it was to begin one.

Most all of the Big Ten coaches had their own method of letting rookies know they had a long way to go to be accepted in the conference.

In his first full year, Showalter was working with veteran referee Art White and it was the rookie's first game at Ohio State. "I made a call that OSU Coach Fred Taylor did not like and he yelled at White, 'Art, where in the hell did you dig up this guy?' He was not speaking to me, so he knew I could do nothing about it, but I got the message."

If Coach Knight became frustrated with a call, he would send his captain over to talk with a referee during a time out.

"There was a play under the IU basket," said Showalter, "and I called it out of bounds instead of a foul. At the time out, over came Kitchel, IU's captain, and said, 'In our last game, the officials at Michigan State called that last play a foul. Why isn't it the same here?' I answered, 'Ted, I wasn't at Michigan State or it would have been the same both places.'"

Helping an out-of-control coach regain his composure played an important part in Showalter becoming friends with Illinois Coach Lou Henson.

"Early in my Big Ten years," said Showalter, "Henson did not like me and it showed. He mellowed a little after the Illinois-Georgia game which I worked in the NCAA tournament. The Illini won in a major upset. But it was the next year that really made the difference.

"Illinois was hooked up in a battle at Iowa and the game ended in a tie, meaning overtime," said the referee. "Midway though the extra period, one of my crew called a foul on an Illinois player and Henson went berserk. He leaped to his feet and started toward the official. I was only a few feet away, so I grabbed him around the chest and held him. He kicked and screamed and kicked and screamed, before finally settling down.

"Illinois won in the second overtime," said Showalter, "and when I kidded Lou about using a bear hug to hold him down, he apologized for his actions. From that day, we have been friends."

Coach Knight would stop to greet the veteran referees as they came onto the floor, but if there was a rookie present, he either totally ignored him or got in some dig.

Rookie Eric Harmon from Monticello was standing next

to veteran Gary Muncy when Knight walked up and shook hands with Showalter and Muncy. Without looking at Harmon he said, "New official, huh. Is he any good?" without batting an eye, Showalter said, "Coach, you will find out in about twenty minutes."

Showalter and Muncy played a practical joke on Harmon in this first game with Knight, with expected results. Showalter told the story:

"Knight knows how long a minute is, without ever looking at the clock. He gets his team back on the floor before the minute expires and he expects the other team to do the same. And Knight hates noise in the huddle. He had the IU official timer's horn moved so it would not blow in his ear.

"So, we told Harmon that Knight was notorious for being late in getting his team back on the floor and the first time the minute was running out, he needed to go to the huddle and blow his whistle to warn him. He did that and Knight came totally unglued. He screamed at Harmon and screamed at Harmon and screamed at Harmon. Eric looked at us in despair and we were breaking up with laughter. He knew he had been had."

Iowa was at Minnesota in the last game of the 1973 season and it seemed certain the Golden Gophers would win at home and beat Indiana for the Big Ten championship. Showalter and Fouty had the game. Showalter told the story.

"Dick Schultz was the Iowa coach and sure enough, at the half, he was getting clobbered, 46-33. As Fouty and I came out of the dressing room for the start of the second half, there stood Schultz in the hallway, outside his team's dressing room door. He was storming. 'I don't care if they ever come to the floor for the second half,' he screamed. 'I am done with this team. They are nothing. Done . . . done . . . done.'

"As happens so many times, the Iowa players came out with fire in their eyes and played like all-stars, sending the game into overtime. As it wound down, Iowa held a one point lead when the Iowa center, Kevin Kunnert, made a tremendous and clean block of the shot that would have won it for the Golden Gophers. It ended in an Iowa victory, 79-77, and was the biggest upset of the year. The Minnesota loss gave IU a tie for the Big Ten championship.

"A few days later," said Showalter, "Schultz received a package in the mail from Bob Knight. Inside was an IU blanket."

Showalter, and his crew of officials, were to work the Southern Mississippi game at Florida State, but when they arrived at the fieldhouse in early afternoon there were no cars. "We went inside and found Coach M.K. Turk from Southern Mississippi, running his players through a drill.

"What time is the game?" asked the head referee.

"It is at 8 o'clock this evening," answered Turk.

"We thought it was this afternoon," admitted Showalter. Turk laughed and said, "How about that! You guys haven't even started to referee and already you have made a major mistake."

Rules of the Big Ten say a referee must arrive one and one-half hours prior to a game and if you do not, you are severely reprimanded. Showalter, who worked four NCAA tournaments, missed the chewing out by a minute. Here is his story:

"I arrived in Detroit in a snowstorm and the airline announced there would be a delay in the flight to East Lansing. I had the IU at Michigan State game and immediately got off the plane. I could not take a chance the delay would make me late. Since I never check a bag when on a flight to referee, I hurried to Hertz to rent a car. Suddenly I remembered I had an extra ticket for the game so I yelled out, 'is anyone going to East Lansing?'

"A man, with a big, black beard, said yes, he was. My dad had always taught me never to trust a man with a beard and I wish I had listened to him. But I grabbed the guy, thinking he already had booked a car, but he had not. Since it was too late to change plans, I rented a car and we headed for East Lansing.

"I was so caught up in trying to get there for the game, I never did ask the guy his name. The roads were horrible and when we finally got to Jenison fieldhouse, there were only thirty minutes left until game time. I told the guy with me that I would leave his ticket at the will-call window and for him to park the car. He said that since I was going home another way, he would be glad to turn the car in for me and I readily agreed, handing him the papers. I ran for the door.

"When I got to the dressing room, I slammed the door shut, grabbed a chair and sat down, twenty-five minutes before we had to go to the floor. Somehow I sensed the Big Ten supervisor of officials would come into that room and sure enough, one minute later, he did.

"He looked at us and said, 'I'm glad you made it. The roads out there are terrible. I wasn't real sure I was going to get here for awhile.' I said, 'yes, sir, they are. We had to struggle to get here an hour and a half ahead of time ourselves.' I thought my partner for the game, Eddie Hightower from Alton, Illinois, would choke to keep from laughing.

"But that is not the end. The next day my phone rang and it was Hertz at Detroit, asking what I had done with their car. I tried to explain but it didn't work. The guy had stolen the car. I knew not to trust a bearded man. Three days later I received my fifth call from Hertz and a woman said, 'Mr. Showalter. The car has been turned in at another Hertz in Michigan and your charge will only be for four days.' It sure beat paying for a new Plymouth Reliant," said the veteran official.

Referees could endear themselves to college coaches by going the extra mile, and they often did so. McBride was no exception. Hope College from Michigan, was to play at Ball State University in Muncie, but a heavy snowstorm hit the northern part of Indiana and lower Michigan. At game time, Hope had not arrived and a call to the college said the team was on its way.

Jim Hinga, the coach at Ball State, knew if the bus reached an impasse in the snow, the Hope coach would let him know, so he decided to keep his team in the gymnasium and wait.

At 10 p.m., and still no Hope team, the Ball State athletic director, Bob Primmer, came to McBride and said, "Mac, we can use referees from our staff when Hope gets here. You do not have to stay."

"No problem, Bob," answered the referee. "I was hired to work this game and I'll stay. I've got nothing else to do." The Hope team arrived a few minutes before midnight and the game ended at 2 A.M.

Jumpin' Johnny Wilson is one of the best players ever to suit up for Anderson College, but you didn't mess with him.

Franklin College had an all-conference center named Fitzpatrick and each time he would hit a hook shot, he would stick it to Wilson with such remarks as, "You hate that, don't you John?"

In the third quarter, Wilson had the ball and Fitzpatrick let him have it in the side with an elbow. The benches emptied as a battle ensued. The two referees finally got it under control and McBride told both centers he had had enough. He told them he was not going to toss them out of the game at that moment, but if they did not settle down and play ball, they both were gone.

Early in the fourth quarter, McBride called a foul on an Anderson guard named Freeman, and as they walked toward the opposite free throw line, he tossed the ball to McBride. But the Anderson guard lost control as he let go of the ball and it sailed over the referee's head and hit a Franklin player in the back. The player turned to Freeman and said, "Hey, you finally found something you can hit."

Freeman popped him and both benches emptied again,

this time a real free-for-all. The referees immediately waded in, tossing bodies right and left, but it took twenty minutes, and outside help, to get it under control. When play was ready to resume, McBride went to the official bench to check with the timer.

"How much time left?" he asked. "Twenty seconds."

"Twenty seconds," cried McBride. "Why didn't you let me know and we would have ended the game with the fight and let them kill each other off."

Referees also could become part of the game without realizing it. And coaches were not beyond taking advantage of any situation. Burl Shook was calling the Hanover-Franklin College game in the early fifties with McBride, when there was a traveling violation at the center line.

On the small Franklin floor, McBride handed the ball to the host team player and stepped to the side, still on the floor. Suddenly he realized the Hanover guard was using him for a screen and as the Franklin player stepped back, he was cut off by the referee. The Hanover player took the toss in, went around McBride and rolled under for two points.

Later in the year, Hanover was playing at Earlham College, Richmond, and they were tied for first place in the Hoosier College Conference. The game was close all the way, with the lead changing hands several times. McBride and Hilligoss were working the game and kept it well under control. With five seconds to go, Earlham appeared to have it won when a Hanover player tossed up an impossible shot that hit nothing but net.

Overtime.

Again the lead changed hands four times and with seconds to go, Hanover had a chance to win it, but missed, and a second overtime was needed. Both teams refused to let the other team get the spurt needed to win and as this period went down to the wire, the game again was tied.

With seven seconds showing on the clock, the ball was passed to Earlham guard Duane Queener, who later coached at Knightstown for many years, and he hesitated for an instant. Queener was standing directly in front of the scorers bench, almost mid court. Even with the roar of the crowd, those at the bench heard McBride say, "Shoot it, kid." He did. Dead center. Earlham won by two points.

After the game a bench official asked McBride why he decided to start coaching. McBride laughingly answered, "John and I are used to working those small high school floors. We are beat."

Woody McBride was the star player for Indiana Central and in a college game at Anderson, the local sports writer, Red Haven, asked Referee McBride if they were related.

"Sure are," answered the official, "he's my cousin and if you think you are going to win tonight you are crazy."

Actually the referee had no idea Indiana Central had a player named McBride until he got to Anderson that night. Woody scored thirty-two points and they clobbered Anderson. Haven was ready to blast the referee in his column when he was told the truth by the Anderson coach.

Not only coaches and referees became friends after the battles of the hardwood, but it also happened many times with ballplayers. Don Barnett was captain of the Anderson Ravens and an excellent player. One of his teammates was Jumpin' Johnny Wilson and the Ravens had been rolling over opponents like a steamroller. But, like often happens, no matter how good a team is, it has an off night and the steamroller ran out of gas at Franklin.

"The Grizzlies also had a fine ball club," said McBride, "and I was expecting a hard-fought contest. Sure enough it was and Franklin upset Anderson in the closing moments. "I was seated in the dressing room after the game when the door opened and Barnett stuck his head in. 'Ref,' he said, 'if I ever get a screwing like that again I sure hope I get kissed.'

"So," said McBride, "I jumped to my feet, hurried to the door, and before he had a chance to close it, I grabbed him and gave him a big kiss on the forehead.

"As we were leaving, the Anderson coach stopped me and wanted to know what I did to his captain? I told him I taught him a lesson in referee-player relations.

"Two weeks later, I had a game at Anderson and when I walked onto the floor here came Barnett with a big smile on his face. 'Mr. McBride,' he said, 'I want to apologize for what happened at Franklin.' I looked at him and asked, 'What was that?' 'Oh, the remark I made to you after the game.' I put my hand on his shoulder and said, 'Son, a good referee does not carry a chip on his shoulder and the remark you made is past history.'"

Barnett looked at McBride and said, "I'll believe that when I see it."

"After the game ended," said the referee, "I was walking off the court when I saw Barnett running toward me. I stopped and could not help but smile when he said, 'Ref, now I believe.'"

When Don Odle was coaching at Taylor University, the old Maytag gymnasium had an overhanging balcony that he used to perfection. And, in the old Hoosier College Conference, Odle ranked with Dutch Struck at Hanover in getting every advantage he could.

John Mutchner, former Rose Hulman coach and athletic director, with tongue in cheek, loves to tell this story.

"Don always had the opposing team bench in under the overhang, so the opponents could not see the scoreboard. In order to check the score, or the time, you had to take one step onto the floor and look up.

"Our game had been a good one from the first jump, and I knew time was getting short. When I checked with my assistant coach concerning the score, we both realized we had lost track of it. So, I started to get up and check the scoreboard, just as the ball came bouncing into my hands.

"As I handed the ball to the referee, I asked, 'what's the score?'

"The referee looked up and said, 'We're leading, 68-64.'"

It was a set-up to get back on an official for all the antics he pulled during his long career. The referee was Charlie Fouty . . . the young woman the fiancee of Rose Hulman's starting center . . . the instigator, John Mutchner, coach of the Engineers. Mutchner had a photographer tipped off to be ready when Fouty was caught totally by surprise. Whistle in his mouth, a look of bewilderment on his face and above all, his dangling arm that seems to say, "I wouldn't touch you with a ten-foot pole,"—this is a classic.

    -Photo courtesy John Mutchner

Referee Cy Birge hands the game ball to Lew Alcindor (Kareem Abdul-Jabbar) after the UCLA great broke the Chicago Stadium scoring record in 1967. UCLA Coach John Wooden, an Indiana native, is at the right with his assistant, Jerry Norman, next to him. UCLA defeated the University of Illinois in a non-conference game.
-Photo courtesy Cy Birge

Big Ten official Bob Showalter, center, discusses a problem with Purdue Coach Gene Keady and Wisconsin Coach Steve Yoder, in this eighties conference game. Referee Eddie Hightower is at left.
-Photo courtesy Meg Theno

The three referees for the 1972 Indiana College All-Star game against the Ohio College All-Stars, posed in the dressing room prior to tip-off. They are, (l-r), Bob Showalter, John Thomas and Gary Muncy. The game was played at Hinkle Fieldhouse.
　　　-Photo courtsey John Thomas

Don McBride worked college games throughout Indiana during his career. This photo tells it all. A basketball, a whistle and a striped shirt, elements that were used to make Indiana number one in the sport of basketball.
　　　-Richmond Palladium-Item *photo*

During a college all-star game at Indianapolis, Coach Ray Meyer of DePaul University tells Referee Bob Showalter he can't see any better wearing glasses. Showalter was the first Big Ten referee to start wearing glasses and took a lot of razzing from coaches and fans for doing so.

    -Photo courtsey Bob Showalter

The family of Homer Owens, Jr., presented him with this photo at the time of his retirement from refereeing in 1976. Although he much preferred high school ball, Owens also officiated college games in Indiana.

    -Photo courtesy Julia Owens

Lowell Smith and Rosalie Leedy worked the final game of the first Girls State Tournament at Hinkle Fieldhouse in 1976. Warsaw defeated Bloomfield, 57-52, for the title. On the twentieth anniversary of that first championship, both teams and both referees were honored between the afternoon games of the 1995 Girls State Tournament at Market Square Arena in Indianapolis.
  -Photo courtesy Lowell Smith

1991

NCAA
BASKETBALL
MEN'S AND WOMEN'S
RULES AND
INTERPRETATIONS

RULE 8

Free Throw

SECTION 1. Positions During Attempt
Play: During the first attempt by A1 of a two free-throw award, B2 does not occupy third lane space and A3 takes it. Before the ball is handed to A1 for the second try, B2 requests permission to occupy the third space. **RULING:** Grant request of B2.

SECTION 2. Who Attempts
Play 1: A2 attempts a free throw that should have been taken by A1. **RULING:** If the attempt by A2 is do to a justifiable misunderstanding, there is no penalty. The error may be corrected under Rule 2-10. If it is reasonable to believe that A2 knew that A1 was the designated shooter, a technical foul for unsporting conduct shall be called. The technical foul will be administered after A1 shoots the free throw to which he or she is entitled.

Play 2: A1 is fouled by B1 and appears injured as a result. The official suspends play at the proper time. Team A indicates it desires a timeout. At the expiration of the timeout, it is apparent that a substitute for A1 is not necessary. Before the signal is given to resume play, A6 reports and is beckoned onto the court by an official. A6 indicates he or she is to replace A1, which would avoid a timeout being charged to Team A. **RULING:** A1 is required to attempt the free throw or throws unless an injury prevents A1 from doing so.

SECTION 5. Ball in Play If Free Throw Is Missed
Play: Team A is assessed with a technical foul. Right after the ball is handed to B1 at the free-throw line by the official, A2 pushes B2 flagrantly. Referee disqualifies A2 from the contest. **RULING:** No players will take positions along the free-throw lane for B1's two free-throw attempts or for B2's two free-throw attempts. Following B2's two free throws, Team B will be awarded the ball for a throw-in at the spot nearest to where the flagrant personal foul was committed.

BI-31

10

Two Winners in One Game

Glen Wisler refereed in college ball for ten years. He was known for his consistent decisions and for taking little guff off any coach during a game.

Even though he was a take-charge referee, he did not call unnecessary fouls and was a favorite on the college circuit.

In the early fifties he was involved in the most bizarre ending of any game during his college refereeing days.

Wisler was working with Tubby Trobaugh at Angola in a game between Tri-State and a technical school from Defiance, Ohio. It was a close game throughout and with twenty seconds to go, Tri scored a basket that showed them with a one-point lead on the scoreboard. The Ohio team worked for a last shot, but it missed.

"We had just started to undress to shower," said Wisler, "when the official scorer and the scoreboard operator came hurrying into the dressing room."

"Fellas, we got a problem," said the official scorer. "The scoreboard showed Tri winning by one point but my scorebook shows Tri getting beat by one point. We've got to resume the game and play it out."

"I looked at Tubby," said Wisler, "for he was the senior referee. He thought for a moment and then said, 'Look men. There is no place to start and no place to end. Tell you what let's do. You,' speaking to the scorer, 'go back to Defiance and report to the newspaper that you won by one point. You,' he said to the scoreboard operator, 'report to the Angola paper that you won by one point. Now, let's go home.'

"It is the only game I ever refereed where we never knew who won," said Wisler.

Many athletic directors and coaches had their own special way to let a referee know whether he was doing a good job or not, without saying so out loud. Hanover's AD, Dutch Struck, may have had the most unique method, and every Indiana referee who worked college games knew about it.

Hanover played in the Hoosier College Conference (HCC) and Struck, who had a foghorn voice and a big heart, always came into the referee dressing room after the game. There was a pop machine there and he would get a bottle of orange drink. If he thought the referees had done a good job he would open the bottle and drink it slowly while amiably chatting with them.

"But if Struck thought you did a poor job," laughed John Thomas, "he would walk into the room without saying a word, get the bottle of pop from the machine and almost bite off the neck of the bottle as he downed it in a couple of gulps. His eyes would glisten as he drank and we kept our mouths shut. When the bottle was empty he would walk out of the room and I must admit we, referees, would give a sigh of relief."

Franklin was playing at Hanover in a mid-fifties HCC contest, when a shot bounced high off the basket and hit the top of the bankboard, rolled along it and fell forward without touching a support or going over the back. Wisler said it was a no call, but the Hanover players quit on the rebound and the Franklin center grabbed it, stuffed it back in and it counted. It proved to be a crucial basket, near the end of the game. Struck, well known for his temper, went bananas.

"Dutch, who could be heard a mile away, screamed at the top of his foghorn lungs," said Wisler. "I simply ignored him and finished the game.

"I had little more than entered the dressing room when in stormed Dutch. He grabbed his usual bottle of pop and squeezed it so hard I am surprised the glass did not break.

He gulped it down in three swigs and then started in on me again. By this time, I was in no mood for more ranting and I ordered him out of the dressing room. When he slammed the door, the hinges surely had to vibrate for five minutes.

"The next day was Sunday," said Wisler, "and Dutch came to Rushville as guest of the Taft family, who were Hanover graduates and owned a furniture store in town. When I walked into church, there he was and we sat near each other. That afternoon we attended a coffee hour in his honor and again sat together and talked basketball.

"Not once, during the entire day, did Dutch mention the call from the night before. It was over and it was forgotten," said Wisler.

Cy Birge worked college games for several years, including eleven in the Big Ten and four NCAA tournaments. But his most unusual experience came in a game at Evansville with Purdue the opponent.

There had been a terrible snowstorm the night before and the Big Ten substituted Roland Baker to work with Birge. The scheduled referee simply could not get there.

"Roland said he would pick me up on the way," said Birge, "but he found he could not due to the drifted roads. So I shoveled my driveway to get my car out, and headed down the road for the fifty-five miles to Evansville. I have never driven in snow like that and soon knew I would be late arriving.

"Tom Yancy from Evansville had worked the preliminary game, so, when I did not arrive, officials decided to have him work with Baker until I got there. When I finally made it to the fieldhouse, I dashed to the dressing room, got ready and headed to the floor.

"The game was going full tilt and Yancy was on my side of the court. He saw me, nodded his head, and as play reached the end where I waited, Yancy left the floor and I stepped in. I've often wondered how many fans in the bleachers even knew the change took place.

"Since Yancy refereed for eight minutes, I offered him part of my check, but he laughingly refused saying, 'No way. Now I got something to tell my grandkids about.'"

A socked-in airport caused Birge a problem with his wife when he took four of his nine children to a game between Illinois and Michigan at Ann Arbor.

"We had no trouble getting there, and it was an excellent game. But when we reached the Detroit airport we found Indianapolis was zero visibility due to fog. However, we were told that if we wanted to take a chance on it clearing by the time we got there, we could go ahead and board, so we did.

"An hour later, we were over Indianapolis and the pilot came on the loudspeaker to say the fog had not lifted and we were going to Memphis, Tennessee. I knew the kids needed to get home so they could go to school the next day and I wondered what my wife would say when I called her. Our conversation went like this:

"Hello, Birge residence."

"Honey, we are going to be a little late getting home. We are in Memphis, Tennessee."

The phone went dead for a moment and then she yelled, "What in the world are you doing in Memphis, Tennessee? You told me you were taking the kids to a game at Ann Arbor, Michigan."

"My wife was very upset," said the Jasper referee, "but the kids loved it. They got to miss a day of school."

Possibly the greatest thrill of Birge's life as a college official came after one of the wildest rides one could have to get to a basketball game. Birge explained:

"Coach John Wooden's UCLA team had Lew Alcindor (Kareem Abdul-Jabbar) at center, and was rated No. 1 in the country. They were playing at the Chicago Stadium in Chicago, Illinois and I had the game. Since this was a rare opportunity to see this great team, I told my family they could go along.

"But the day before the game, we had a huge snowfall and

Coach John Wooden Ranks No. 1

Don McBride, Cy Birge, Bob Showalter, Charlie Fouty and Glen Wisler are in agreement that John Wooden ranks at the top of a long list of fine coaches who plied their trade during the Golden Age.

Wisler said, "Although Wooden became the greatest coach in history, it took him sixteen years at UCLA before he made it past the first round of the NCAA tournament. It seems impossible that his last NCAA championship was in 1975."

Fouty had this to say about the 1973 NCAA victory by UCLA. "Coach Wooden won his seventh consecutive NCAA tournament title that year and his big center, Bill Walton, was outstanding. In fact, Walton was the only member of the Bruins to be named to the all-Final Four team. The game was a total blowout by UCLA, beating Memphis State by twenty-one points."

Showalter came up with an observation concerning the Final Four showdown. He said, "We often talk about the NCAA Final Four championship growing in popularity. Television has been instrumental in this growth. But in my memory there never will be more hype, more speculation, more sheer drama than the confrontation in 1979 between Magic Johnson and Larry Bird. Michigan State won the championship over Indiana State but Larry Bird won the hearts of Indiana basketball fans."

Birge, who refereed the 1967 game between UCLA and Illinois the night Lew Alcindor (Kareem Abdul-Jabbar) broke the single game scoring record, also talked about Coach Wooden. He said, "I doubt if Wooden's record of seven NCAA championships in a row will ever be broken. Those victories years were 1967 through 1973. But Wooden also led UCLA to two consecutive wins in 1964 and 1965. It was a great honor to work games for him."

Don McBride remembered Wooden's Indiana roots. "He was the leading scorer in 1927 when his Martinsville team beat Muncie Central for the state title. He coached high school basketball in Indiana at South Bend Central before entering the college ranks at Indiana State. John Wooden is a true gentleman."

roads were blocked. Somehow I made it to the train depot and we caught a train for the Windy City. Since it was going to be close on time, I dressed for the game on the train.

"When we arrived at the depot in Chicago, I hurried to a telephone to check on the game while my wife took the children outside to get a taxicab. To her surprise, none was available. The snow was too deep for them to move. Just then a truck drove up to deliver newspapers and my wife called to the driver as he got out of the cab."

"Mister," she said, "we need a ride. Is there any chance you could help us out?"

"Where do you need to go?"

"To the Sheraton downtown."

"Well lady," said the driver, "I'm going that way if you don't mind riding in the back of the truck."

Just then her husband came out the door and when she told him the circumstances, they all piled into the back of the truck and made it to the hotel . . . cold, but without further incident.

The game, postponed until the next evening, was all UCLA. Alcindor set a new Chicago Stadium scoring record and Birge had the privilege of presenting him with the game ball at the close of the contest. *The Chicago Tribune* took a photograph of the presentation, and it hangs in a prime location in the Birge home. Coach Wooden can be seen in the picture next to assistant coach Jerry Norman.

But one member of the family missed this great moment for the Jasper referee. Birge's wife was so disgusted with battling the snow that she stayed in the hotel room and didn't attend.

How does a referee feel when he blows a call, especially when the blown call is caught by the greatest coach in basketball history, John Wooden? Glen Wisler said the answer is simple. "I admitted I was wrong."

"UCLA was playing at Butler and Bill Walton was at center. A Butler player shot and Walton went elbows above the basket to block the ball. I called goaltending. But as I blew my whistle I realized Walton had not touched the ball, the shot simply had missed.

"Going to the dressing room at halftime, Wooden fell in step with me and said, 'My man never touched that ball.' 'Yes, sir,'" answered Wisler, 'I know. But I didn't catch it quick enough.'"

"After the game, Wooden came to the dressing room and told us we worked a good game. Then he looked at me and said with a grin, 'Wisler, you are the first referee I have ever seen who admitted he made a mistake.'"

Wisler was working at Manchester College on a Tuesday night, so he stopped by his sister's beauty shop for a quick trim on his butch haircut.

"She got her clippers, put on the clip for a butch and started down my head. Suddenly the clip flew off and before she could stop she had scalped me. I looked horrible. So she got an eyebrow pencil and filled in the sheared place and I headed to the game.

"I wanted to be at my best that night because pole vaulter Bob Richards and baseball manager Walter Alston were guests of Manchester Coach Claud Wolfe for the game. Mickey McNaught was working it with me.

"Five minutes into the first half, Manchester called a timeout and I saw Wolfe walking toward me, taking a towel from around his neck as he approached. 'Glen,' he said, 'you need this a lot worse than I do.' It was then I realized the black from the eyebrow pencil was running down my face in streaks.

"It was one of the most embarrassing moments of my life."

Wabash College Coach Bill Pedin and Wisler were friends, but the referee caught him totally by surprise with one statement during a late fifties game.

"The contest was barely underway when Bill started yelling, 'number 24 is pushing . . . number 24 is pushing.' I ignored him," said Wisler, "until the start of the second quarter. It was then Pedin sent in a player from his bench wearing the same number 24.

"Down the floor we came and as I passed the Wabash bench, Bill again yelled, 'number 24 is pushing . . . number 24 is pushing.' So I blew the whistle, walked over to him and asked, 'Bill, which 24 is it?' You could have heard a pin drop in that gymnasium for several seconds before Bill realized he had been had. His answer was heard in the far corners of the gym, and the crowd roared, 'Theirs, you damn nut, theirs.' "

Wisler was calling the Eastern Illinois game at Indiana State and the visiting coach was a towering 6'-8". As play progressed, the coach got madder and madder. Finally, with two minutes to go in the half, he motioned the referee to him.

"I walked over and said, 'do we have a problem coach?'

"I don't think he even heard me, for he was screaming at the top of his lungs and his face was stark white. It struck me funny and I smiled at him. This caused him to stop screaming and he said, 'Ref, don't you ever get mad?' I said, 'no sir, for if I did, there would be two horses behinds standing here instead of one. So, let's play basketball.'

"A few weeks later I got a letter from him wanting me to referee a home game in Illinois, but I had to decline due to the distance from my home. I must admit, getting the invitation made me feel good," said the referee.

John Thomas worked the Ohio Valley Conference (OVC) for several years, as well as the Hoosier College Conference and independent teams such as Notre Dame and Dayton. He was considered one of the very best.

"It always was interesting to go to Morehead State, down in Kentucky," said the Shelbyville referee, "for two reasons. One, the athletic director's wife played the organ before the game, during timeouts and at halftime. She always greeted the referees with the tune, *Three Blind Mice*. Naturally the crowd reacted to this with a roar of approval and the referees tried to ignore the whole thing.

"Two, the entire floor was surrounded by folding chairs, stretching each direction from the two player benches and the scorer's table. These were Morehead faculty seats and there were times when they could get quite vocal."

Thomas continued: "Tennessee Tech, with Ken Trickey coaching, was the opponent for Coach Bill Harrell [Muncie Central coach for several years] and the Hilltoppers. Ralph Stout was working with me and there was a rule that if a player lost a contact lens, play must immediately be suspended until it was found.

"I was the trail official and I saw this Tech player throw up his hands like he was trying to catch something and I knew it was a contact lens. So, I blew play dead. If you get on your hands and knees to look for a lens, often the lights will reflect off it and that was what I did, along with a couple of players.

"I was only six feet or so from the sideline when I realized one of the faculty members, who had been on me pretty good, was saying something to me. I looked up and he was handing me his glasses.

"He said, 'Hell ref, you will never find that lens unless you put on these glasses, no better than you can see.' I reached over, took them from him, put them on and at that moment the player found his lens. I jumped to my feet and realized I could barely see through the lens of the glasses, but I was not about to hand them back to the man at that moment. I finished the half wearing the out-of-focus glasses. As I readied to leave the floor, I walked over to the faculty member, handed him the glasses and said, 'you know, you might be right.' He grinned and I had no more problems with him.

"Stout was an excellent referee," said Thomas, "and was capable of handling all situations. We were at Tennessee Tech this time, down at Cookeville, and they were playing a Division I team from Texas. One of the visiting players griped on every call, sometimes throwing his arms in the air in an act of desperation. His tactics had also got his coach and teammates into it and we really were taking some hard knocks.

"Two minutes before the half, Stout called a charging foul on this kid and he went into his 'Oscar' act. He hit the floor, stretched out full length and you could have heard his moan throughout the entire fieldhouse. Ralph hurried to where the player lay, got down on both knees by his side and said, 'Son, if you are not up from there in three seconds, it is a technical foul . . . one thousand one, one thousand two,' and the boy was all legs and arms as he leaped to his feet, beating the time limit. The young man was a perfect gentleman the remainder of the game."

Thomas got stuck with refereeing a college game between Western Kentucky and East Tennessee State by himself when snow kept the second referee from arriving. Here is his story:

"The game was at Bowling Green and Gene Bennett from Cincinnati was to work it with me. I later found out he flew from Cincinnati to Nashville, but the roads to Bowling Green were drifted shut so he could not get out of the airport. When we got the call from Gene, I got the two coaches, Johnny Oldham at Western and Madison Brooks from East Tennessee, together and told them I would do the best I could under the circumstances.

"It turned out to be an excellent game and I worked it from foul line to foul line. However, I wondered if I could get through the final five minutes, I was so dead tired. But I made it.

"After the game, Mr. Hornbeck, the athletic director at Bowling Green, came into the dressing room and thanked me for a job well done. He then said, 'I know Art Guepe [commissioner of the OVC] probably wouldn't agree with this, but we are going to give you Gene's check as well as your own.' It was the only time in my life I ever received double pay for a game."

Roy Gardner was working with Thomas in a Missouri

Valley Conference (MVC) game at Evansville and the opponent was Southern Illinois. Without wanting to, Gardner became part of the action and Evansville Coach Arad McCutcheon tried to sign him up.

"Evansville all-star, Jerry Sloan, grabbed a rebound," said Thomas, "saw Larry Humes open at the other end of the floor and threw a long pass. Roy was racing down court to cover and had his back turned. The ball hit him in the left shoulder, careened into the air, right into the hands of fast breaking Buster Briley and he laid it up for two points.

"At the half I went to the scorer's bench and told them to be sure and put down Roy for an assist. McCutcheon told him a scholarship was available. Roy, although embarrassed, took it all in good humor."

Thomas considers Bailey Robertson, Oscar's older brother, one of the best college players he saw in action, and one who loved to infuriate his coach at Indiana Central, Angus Nicoson.

"Central was hosting Coach Don Odle and his Taylor Trojans," recalled Thomas, "and, as usual, it was an excellent game, close all the way. Everyone connected with Indiana Central knew of Nicoson's temper, and in fact, behind his back he was known as Angry Angus.

"The game was in the old Central fieldhouse, and the benches on which the players sat were held up by wide legs some three feet from the end of the board, one at each end. Bailey pulled a boner on the floor and Angus jerked him out. He proceeded to give his star player a tongue lashing and told him to go sit on the other end of the bench, he wanted nothing to do with him.

"Bailey did as he was told, but when he sat down he realized his coach had made the other players on the bench scoot away from his star, isolating him from the rest of the team. Nicoson had settled in his seat, and play started to resume, when I heard this terrible commotion. I looked toward the sideline just in time to see five players and one coach go sliding off the end of the bench. Bailey, realizing his weight was all that was keeping it stable, stood up. It made a perfect slide."

Thomas had a game in the Indiana-Kentucky All-Star college series soon after the three-point rule had gone into effect. Johnny Dee, the Notre Dame coach, was the all-star mentor, and he had a boy on the team from his school who was an excellent long shot.

"Late in the second half, the game really tightened up," said Thomas, "and this kid set himself with his toe on the three-point line and fired away. It hit dead center but I called it two points, pointing to the line."

"Hey Thomas," yelled Dee. "That's three points in South Bend. Why isn't it down here?"

Thomas yelled back, "Because they don't use a one-inch brush to make the line down here, like you do in South Bend."

He said the coach laughed, threw his hand at him as if to say you win, and the game continued without incident.

Lowell Smith enjoyed working college ball and refereed often for the University of Evansville. Buster Briley, a former star at Madison and now the leading scorer for Evansville, tried pulling a fast one that backfired.

"Bob Laird and I had the game and Evansville had a powerhouse. But DePauw had a good record, and we thought it might be close. Midway through the last half, I called a foul on a DePauw player, turned and walked to the line and there stood Buster. I looked at him and said, 'Buster, you are not supposed to be here.' 'Yes sir, I am,' he answered. I went over to Laird and asked him, but he did not know.

"So, I went back to the line, taking my time, since I expected the DePauw coach to let me know I had the wrong shooter. Nothing happened. So, again I said, 'Buster, you know you are not supposed to be here.' 'Yes sir, Mr. Ref,' he answered, 'I'm the shooter.'

"I shrugged my shoulders, handed him the ball and backed off. Briley was hitting eight-five per cent or so of his free throws, so I thought it would be automatic. He missed. I grabbed the ball and as I handed it to him I said, 'see what you get for not being the right shooter.' Again he said, 'Yes sir, Mr. Ref, I'm the shooter.' I stepped back and he missed his second try.

"Evansville won the game easily. As I walk out of the dressing room to head home, there stood Buster. He grinned at me and said, 'Mr. Smith, I won't ever do that anymore when you are refereeing, I promise.' Before I could answer, he turned and hurried away."

College games can get totally out of hand unless the referees take charge and do so early. In the game between Evansville and North Carolina A&T, it was smooth until four minutes were left to play. Smith recalls what happened:

"This was the last game of the season for A&T, plus the last game the team would play that would count in the league standings since several violations had resulted in the NCAA giving the North Carolina team a two-year suspension.

"Paul Biebel from Chicago was working with me and Evansville was up by five on its home court, with four minutes to play.

On a foul violation I said to Paul, I sure hope this stays close or it is going to be slaughter. It didn't stay close. Evansville ran off six quick points, and from that moment on, every time an Evansville player touched a ball, he was clobbered by an A&T player.

"We called personal fouls. We called flagrant fouls. We called technical fouls. None of it did any good. I wonder if we should have terminated the game on the basis someone might get hurt, but we played it out. There is no doubt," he said, "it was the hardest four minutes of refereeing I had during my career."

At least one of Indiana's top high school referees found college games were not for him. Dick Jacobs worked one year of college ball, but a policeman at Louisville and two deer caused him to end his college career before it hardly got started.

"Twice in that one year," said Dick, "I hit deer on my way home from a college game and each time I destroyed my car. Fortunately, I was not hurt either time, but I was lucky.

"As for the policeman," he continued, "I was working a game at the University of Louisville and since it was my first time there, I asked this officer where I was to park. He directed me to a place near the fieldhouse, so I got my equipment out of the car, locked it and headed into the game.

"After it was over," continued Jacobs, "I dressed, picked up my check, walked out to where I had parked and my car was gone. I thought it must have been stolen so I hurried over to a police car sitting by the entrance and told the officer what had happened. He informed me that my car was parked in an illegal zone and had been towed away. When I tried to explain I had been told to park there, he rolled up the window of his car."

It took the referee two hours, plus paying a hefty fine and the tow bill, before he was able to get his car. "As I drove away from the yard where my car had been towed, I said out loud, 'no more, no more.' So I went back to high school refereeing and never regretted the move," Jacobs said.

The college circuit was extremely hard for referees, even during the Golden Age, due to traveling great distances to games, refereeing unmatched competition and surviving the general format of the game itself. Coaches demanded more than those in high school. Fans often blamed the referees when their team was playing poorly. Yet, there also were many rewards and you will find few referees who regret their years working college competition.

But the Golden Age also has ended for college referees. Fouty, Showalter, McBride, Wisler, Birge, Smith and Thomas are unanimous in believing the love of the game has been lost, except for a very few. Fouty said it best with these words, "Today it is all business. They learn the rules, they demand obedience and use the technical as a sword hanging over each player and bench. They are afraid to call the flagrant foul and if there is a questionable call, the home court team will get the decision. It is time for some revamping . . . no . . . it is past time."

The referees of the Golden Age have spoken. They have seen the good and the bad. They look back with no regrets. So, in Indiana, what could be more fitting to close than having a veteran referee tell one more Bob Knight story. It begins far from the IU gymnasium, and Don McBride, who has never been a Coach Knight fan, is the narrator.

"Lou Kenworthy lived in Richmond for several years, and after moving to Dayton, Ohio, became IU's ambassador in that city. He had a sign in his driveway that said, 'Parking For IU Fans Only.' He never missed an IU game on TV, and when it came to statistics, he had them all. His family room, the room where he spent most of his time during the final months of his battle with cancer, had IU books and pictures all over the place.

"Lou had a friend who played briefly in the professional ranks and knew how badly his buddy wanted to see an IU game. But for Lou, going to IU for a game was an impossible dream since he could not climb stairs and tickets were incredibly hard to get. He, long ago, had put the idea of ever going out of his head.

"Then one day, during the basketball season, the doorbell rang and Lou hobbled to answer it. There stood former Dayton Coach Don Donoher. 'Lou,' he said, 'I understand you would like to see IU play.' 'More than anything in this world,' Lou answered. 'Well,' said Donoher, 'I have been talking to Coach Knight and he wants you and your wife to be his guest at a game. Here is his private telephone number. Phone him at 4 o'clock this afternoon and he will set it up.'

"Lou was flabbergasted. He did call the number and Knight answered. He told Lou to pick the date and let him know. There would be four tickets waiting for him, so someone else could drive, and four chairs on the floor next to former IU great Landon Turner's permanent spot for all games. [Turner, after being severely injured in an automobile accident as mentioned earlier, sits in his wheelchair on the floor, near the entrance where the IU team enters].

"Lou, his wife Barbara, and another couple did go. When they entered the fieldhouse three hours before game time, as instructed, Knight was there to greet them. He chatted for some five minutes and told them of a good restaurant nearby.

"Upon returning to the gymnasium, Lou found his seat next to Landon Turner and they immediately hit it off, for Lou never met a stranger. When Knight came on the floor, he stopped to check and see if everything was all right with Lou and his party.

"Lou said the next couple hours were the greatest moments of his life as he watched his beloved Hoosiers win in a close contest. As Knight left the floor he gave Lou a 'high five' and the Dayton man said he could have floated out to the car.

"But it doesn't end there. A couple days later the phone rang at Dayton and Lou answered. 'Lou,' said a familiar voice, 'this is Bob Knight. I wanted to check and see if you enjoyed your visit and to tell you I am sending you a couple of items in the mail.'

"The next afternoon a UPS truck drove into the driveway and when Lou opened the package, there was an IU clock, an autographed picture of Coach Knight and an IU banner.

"On the day he died, Lou had these three items within eyesight of his bed. Bob Knight will never know the joy he gave this dying man in those final weeks when all the world looked bleak."

— 30 —

Referees and Umpires

Each of these referees was interviewed, with the exception of John Hilligoss, who is deceased. Both C.N. Phillips and Joe Mullins have died since the author talked with them. Each referee, with the exception of Rosalie Leedy, worked with Don McBride. Two coaches and one player also were interviewed and are listed below. Until 1959, the lead official in a game was called the referee and the second official the umpire. Therein the reason for using the Referees title for those interviewed and the Umpires title for those who were not.

REFEREES

Don McBride, Richmond. Graduate Richmond High School 1935. Officiated 1935-1963. State Finals 1951-52. Silver Medal Winner, Indiana Basketball Hall of Fame 1987.

John Hilligoss, Richmond (deceased). Graduate Centerville High School 1934. Officiated 1936-1964. State Finals 1952-53.

Cyril (Cy) Birge, Jasper. Graduate Jasper High School 1934. Officiated 1939-1971. State Finals 1951-52-54. Big Ten Referee 1959-1969. Officiated in NCAA Tournament four years. Member of Indiana Basketball Hall of Fame 1995.

Karl Bly, Connersville. Graduate Kendallville High School 1935. Officiated 1947-1963.

Everett (Scoop) Campbell, Dunkirk. Graduate Dunkirk High School 1943. Officiated 1943-1970. State Finals 1962-63-64.

Charlie Fouty, Terre Haute. Graduate Indiana State Laboratory High School 1946. Officiated 1948-1980. State Finals 1964-65. Assigned NCAA Finals 1968-69-71-76-77. Indiana Basketball Hall of Fame 1980.

Danny Jacobs, Ellettsville. Graduate Stinesville High School 1949. Officiated 1955-1980. State Finals 1980.

Winfield (Dick) Jacobs, Ellettsville. Graduate Stinesville High School 1943. Officiated 1947-1982. State Finals 1962-63-64.

Rosalie (Rosie) Leedy, Indianapolis. Graduate Ben Davis High School 1956. Officiated 1975-1977. Refereed first Girls State Finals game in 1976, afternoon finals game in 1977.

Fred Marlow, Rushville. Graduate Sandusky High School 1940. Officiated 1949-1972.

William (Bill) May, Richmond. Graduate Hagerstown High School 1951. Officiated 1951-1974. State Finals 1972-73-74.

Joseph (Joe) Mullins, (deceased) Kokomo. Graduate Bunker Hill High School 1934. Officiated 1939-1964. State Finals 1957-58.

John Mutchner, Terre Haute. Graduate Lynn High School 1949. One of the best small college coaches in Indiana history. Coached twenty three years at Rose Hulman.

Charlie Northam, Portland. Graduate Arlington High School 1939. Officiated 1941-1963. State Finals 1956-57. Refereed final game when Crispus Attucks won state and finished undefeated.

Homer (Junior) Owens, Modoc. Graduate Huntsville High School 1943. Officiated 1943-1976. State Finals 1965-66-67.

C.N. Phillips, Greencastle (deceased). Graduate Fillmore High School 1929. Officiated 1929-1949. State Finals 1945-46-49.

Howard Plough, Connersville. Graduate Connersville High school 1937. Officiated 1940-1963.

Bobby Plump, Indianapolis. Graduate Milan High School 1954. Trester Award Winner 1954. Member Basketball Hall of Fame 1981.

Frank Sanders, Claypool. Graduate Claypool High School 1937. Officiated 1939-1963. State Finals 1959-60.

Howard Sharpe, Terre Haute. Coached 1940-1987. Holds state record for games won, 753, while losing 345, a .686 percentage. Had record of 486 wins, 186 losses as coach of Terre Haute Gerstmeyer. National Coach of the Year in 1975. Inducted Indiana Basketball Hall of Fame 1971.

Robert (Bob) Showalter, New Castle. Graduate Fountain City High School 1953. Officiated 1954-1987. State Finals 1970-71. Big Ten Referee 1971-1987. Officiated in five NCAA Tournaments. Officiated last state final game held at Hinkle Fieldhouse.

Lowell Smith, Palmyra. Graduate Morgan Township High School 1953. Officiated 1953-1979. State Finals 1972-73. Girls State Finals 1976-77. Only referee in state to work championship game in all four finals.

Don Snedeker, Connersville. Graduate Alquina High School 1948. Officiated 1953-1983. State Finals 1980.

Robert (Bob) Spay, Kokomo. Graduate Tipton High School 1938. Officiated 1946-1966. State Finals 1964-65.

John Thomas, Shelbyville. Graduate Fairland High School 1944. Officiated 1947-1975. Had three semistates.

Glen Wisler, Denver. Graduate Chili High School 1940. Officiated 1941-1969. State Finals 1967-68.

UMPIRES

The following referees are to be found in the book. Some were outstanding. Others were only mediocre. But all gave their best. None was interviewed. Several are deceased.

Many did not work with Don McBride but are named due to working with at least one of the twenty-two listed under Referees.

Frank Baird, Indianapolis, Indiana Basketball Hall of Fame 1974; Griz Baker, Franklin; Tom Baker, Anderson; Wendell Baker, Indianapolis; Ernie Baldwin, Muncie; Odie Barnett, Muncie (deceased); Bob Beeson, Connersville; George Bender, Indianapolis (Deceased); Bill Berry, Richmond; Kenneth Blankenbaker, Greenwood; Carl Burt, North Manchester; Gene Butts, Warsaw; Gabby Byers, Odon; Don Call, Martinsville (deceased); Frank Carnes, Muncie (deceased); Wayne Crispen, Kokomo.

Jim Davis, Connersville; Karl Dickerson, Crawfordsville, Indiana Basketball Hall of Fame 1983 (deceased); Cliff Dickman, Richmond; Jimmy Dimitroff, Indianapolis; Ross Dorsett, Batesville; Stan Dubis, East Chicago (deceased); Roger Emmert, Haubstadt; Bill Findling, Windfall; Bob Fisher, Farmland (deceased); Carl Fleetwood, Connersville (deceased); Jim Frey, Fort Wayne; Gail Gaddis, Muncie; Charles (Pup) Garber, Bunker Hill; Roy Gardner, Batesville (deceased); Bill Graham, Connersville (deceased); Art Gross, Marion.

John Gwin, Connersville (deceased); Dave Habegger, Berne; Eric Harmon, Monticello; Bob Henne, Albion; Bill Hile, Logansport; John Hilligoss, New Albany; Wayne Hinchman, Winchester; Bob Hoffman, Jasper, Silver Medal Winner, Indiana Basketball Hall of Fame 1980 (deceased); Troy Ingram, Richmond; Maurice (Pete) Jordan, Richmond (deceased); Nate Kaufman, Shelbyville (deceased); Jim Ladd, Williamsburg; Bob Laird, Shelbyville; Bill Larkin, Winamac; John Lemon, Richmond (deceased); Eugene Linn, Gas City; John Magnabosco, Muncie (deceased); Dean Malaska, Indianapolis (deceased); Gene Marks, North Judson.

Wilbur May, Richmond; Darrel McFall, Carmel; Walt McFatridge, Kokomo, IHSAA Medal Winner 1944 (next year called Trester Award); Roger McGriff, Shelbyville; H.P. (Mickey) McNaught, Logansport; Gene McNutt, Williamsburg (deceased); John Lowell (Buz) Mertz, Summitville; Munk McKee, Henryville; Gary Muncy, Fort Wayne; Wes Oler, Economy; Jack O'Neal, Indianapolis (deceased); Rick Owens, Modoc; Jim Patterson, Fairland (deceased).

Dominic Polizotto, Gary (deceased); Jim Ridge, Greens Fork (deceased); Gail (Clab) Robinson, Connersville (deceased); Oscar Samuels, Frankton (deceased); Frank Shamel, Cambridge City (deceased); Norm Shields, Bloomington; Merle Shively, Warsaw; Burl Shook, Richmond; Ed Straithmiller, Indianapolis; Charlie Stump, Rushville (deceased); Walter Thurston, Mishawaka (deceased); Marvin Todd, Fort Wayne (deceased); Raymond (Tubby) Trobaugh, Angola (deceased); Bob Wells, Shelbyville (deceased); Fred White, Columbia City; Dee Williams, Brazil, member Indiana Basketball Hall of Fame.

THE PRINCIPALS

These men made basketball king in Indiana. Their lives were dedicated to the sport and they worked tirelessly to see rules were followed, the game's integrity upheld and referees and coaches alike toed the mark. They also were ready to assist at any time to keep basketball Indiana's No. 1 sport.

Arthur L. Trester. Commissioner of the IHSAA from 1929-1944. First of the Indiana basketball czars. Trester, deceased, was elected a Silver Medal Winner, Indiana Basketball Hall of Fame in 1965.

L. V. Phillips, commissioner of the IHSAA from 1945 to 1962. His word was law. Now deceased, Phillips was elected a Silver Medal Winner, Indiana Basketball Hall of Fame in 1963.

Phillip (Phil) Eskew, commissioner 1962 to 1976. Had a tremendous pair of shoes to fill when Phillips retired but was outstanding in his position. Eskew, who is deceased, was the Silver Medal Winner, Indiana Basketball Hall of Fame, 1970.

Robert (Cobbie) Hinshaw, assistant commissioner and the man who did the ground work for the IHSAA. Elected to the Indiana Basketball Hall of Fame in 1963. He is deceased.

Herman Keller, assistance commissioner from 1961-1973. He was named to the Indiana Basketballl Hall of Fame in 1965. Keller is deceased.

Charlie Maas, assistant commissioner from 1973-1984. Maas, deceased, was elected to the Indiana Basketball Hall of Fame in 1985.

Tony Hinkle, referee and coach. Was host for IHSAA tournament finals and advisor to all state referees and coaches. Coached at Butler University and fieldhouse was changed from Butler Fieldhouse to Hinkle Fieldhouse in his honor. He is deceased.

Max Knight has done it all — or at least tried to. He became a veteran pilot at age ten (his father owned an airport); served in the cavalry during World War II; went to Earlham College on the GI Bill; was sports editor at Winchester, Indiana; served as editor of the weekly *Lynn Herald* and was for twenty-two years on the staff of the *Richmond Palladium-Item,* first as sports writer-editor and later district feature writer. After "retiring," he entered the ministry and earned two degrees from Bible colleges, then photographed worldwide travelogue movies for ten years, and became a state police chaplain. Active in social and philanthropic organizations, Max has been married to the former Mazella Wright for fifty years. They have two children and three grandchildren.